Judicial Self-Interest

JUDICIAL SELF-INTEREST

Federal Judges and Court Administration

Christopher E. Smith

Westport, Connecticut
London

Library of Congress Cataloging-in-Publication Data

Smith, Christopher E.
    Judicial self-interest : federal judges and court administration /
    Christopher E. Smith.
       p.   cm.
    Includes bibliographical references and index.
    ISBN 0–275–95216–9 (alk. paper)
    1. Judges—United States. 2. Court administration—United States.
    3. Self-interest. I. Title.
    KF8775.S62 1995
    347.73'13—dc20
    [347.30713]   95–3342

British Library Cataloguing in Publication Data is available.

Library of Congress Catalog Card Number: 95–3342
ISBN: 0–275–95216–9

First published in 1995

Praeger Publishers, 88 Post Road West, Westport, CT 06881
An imprint of Greenwood Publishing Group, Inc.

Printed in the United States of America

The paper used in this book complies with the
Permanent Paper Standard issued by the National
Information Standards Organization (Z39.48–1984).

10 9 8 7 6 5 4 3 2 1

For Frances E. Payne and
in memory of C. Edward Payne and
Esther Burdette Smith

Contents

Preface

Scholars face difficulties when writing about authoritative institutions and the people within those institutions who wield power. The desire to provide penetrating criticism and analysis may be tempered by the fear that adverse reactions from powerful individuals may preclude future opportunities to gain the access and information necessary for additional analyses. The courts can be a particularly daunting target for scholarly analysis. Because of the strong desire by insiders to maintain the neutral image and legitimacy of the judicial branch, critical analyses, especially those that reveal the political aspects of courts and law, may be particularly unwelcome. Despite the discomfort caused for some judges and law professors by the study of judicial politics, such analyses are necessary for placing judicial institutions into their proper social and political context.

Critics and defenders of contemporary courts share the goal of improving courts' capacity to fulfill the fundamental responsibilities of the judicial branch. There are obviously widespread disagreements about whether improvements should emphasize efficiency, due process, or other values. However, no matter which elements of the judicial process that any commentator identifies as requiring improvement, reform can be planned and undertaken only with an accurate understanding of how the judicial branch actually operates. This book aspires to be a step, and an admittedly small one at that, toward increasing understanding of the judicial branch by focusing on the role of judges' self-interest in shaping court reform and judicial policies.

I owe many debts of gratitude to people who contributed to my work on this book. None of them bears responsibility for my conclusions, and, indeed, none of them probably agrees with everything that I have written here. In various ways, however, they contributed to the development of my analysis and conclusions. I am especially indebted to various federal judicial officers in scattered U.S. district courts who have provided information about the judicial branch and its operations. George F. Cole of the University of Connecticut stimulated my interest in studying the federal courts. John Green of the University of Akron referred me to literature on interest groups. Avis Alexandria Jones of the University of Maryland worked with me on my initial explorations of habeas corpus reform, and I am grateful to the *Connecticut Law Review* for providing an outlet for those explorations in "The Rehnquist Court's Activism and the Risk of Injustice," 26 (1993): 53–77. Portions of Chapters 2 and 3 are drawn from my previously published work: "Judicial Lobbying and Court Reform: U.S. Magistrate Judges and the Judicial Improvements Act of 1990," *University of Arkansas–Little Rock Law Journal* 14 (1992): 163–198; "Federal Judicial Salaries: A Critical Appraisal," *Temple Law Review* 62 (1989): 849–873. I am grateful to these law reviews for permission to incorporate portions of these published articles into the chapters of this book.

I gained from my parents, Professors Carol Payne Smith and Robert Lee Smith of Western Michigan University, a recognition that one must view human institutions with a critical eye in order to make contributions toward their improvement. Some might say that this was a lesson learned "too well," but I prefer to believe that there is greater value in ruffling a few feathers by raising new questions than in deferring to accepted practices and values. My long-suffering spouse, Charlotte, and children, Alicia and Eric, deserve medals for tolerating my penchant for spending many hours away from them engrossed in my computer and its keyboard.

This book is dedicated, with gratitude, to my grandparents as representatives and embodiments of my forebears whose thankless toil in the difficult settings of farms, coal mines, slaughterhouses, and railroads made possible the education, achievements, and material comforts of their children, grandchildren, and great-grandchildren. While the specific details of court reform and its impact on American society might not have been of great interest to them, they were always dedicated, in their own ways, to the nation's broader, related goal of improving the lives of succeeding generations.

1

Federal Judges and Court Administration

Federal judges are exceptionally powerful actors in the American governing system. Article III of the United States Constitution effectively grants these judges life tenure by declaring that they "shall hold their Offices during good Behaviour."[1] The judges' protected tenure was intended to insulate their judicial decision making from partisan political pressures, and, indeed, it gives them more opportunities for independence than nearly any other officials who work in democratic governing systems. In addition, federal judges embody a co-equal branch of government because they possess the power of "judicial review." Unlike in other democratic systems in which the legislature or executive is supreme, judges in the American federal judiciary possess the authority to invalidate the decisions and actions of legislative and executive officials by declaring those actions to be unconstitutional.

The structural elements of tenure and judicial review that make American federal judges especially powerful are enhanced by the nature of judicial officers' power over constitutional interpretation. Because the United States Constitution is a relatively brief document with numerous ambiguous phrases, judges are able to define and change the Constitution's meaning and thereby shape the distribution of power among the branches of government as well as expand or contract the civil rights and liberties enjoyed by the American citizenry.

Federal judges have used their special attributes, protected tenure, power of judicial review, and authority over constitutional interpretation to make significant decisions affecting public policies that have touched the lives of every American. These key elements of the federal judiciary's extraordinary powers were among the essential factors underlying the United States Supreme Court's controversial 1954 decision to invalidate racial segregation in public schools[2] and the succeeding three decades' worth of decisions by federal lower-court judges that implemented busing to achieve desegregation.[3] Similarly, judges' independence and their authority over judicial review and constitutional interpretation produced controversial and politically unpopular decisions affecting such issues as criminal defendants' rights,[4] prayer in public schools,[5] prisoners' rights,[6] and flag burning as a form of symbolic speech.[7]

During the Warren Court era (1953–1969), in which the Supreme Court led the federal judiciary to produce "what can only be described as a constitutional revolution generated by a group of justices who were perhaps the most liberal in history,"[8] scholars began to focus increasing attention on the power and impact of the judicial branch within the American governing system. Because many of these judicial decisions, especially those addressing racial discrimination, attempted to combat visible injustices, commentators frequently lauded the courts for taking courageous action.

Although much of the literature on the judiciary's impact on the governing system treats judges as powerful policy makers, closer examinations of judicial policy making refined scholars' understanding of the judicial branch by demonstrating that judges were less powerful than they appeared to be. For example, Charles Johnson and Bradley Canon explained how federal judges lack the ability to implement their policy decisions.[9] Judges can issue declarations about what ought to occur, but the actual implementation of judicial policy rests in the hands of lower judicial and executive officials who must interpret and carry out judicial orders. Similarly, Gerald Rosenberg found that many public policies that were presumed to flow from judicial decisions actually took shape only after other governmental actors endorsed and enforced the original judicial directives.[10] Although the Supreme Court declared in 1954 that racial segregation in schools violated the Constitution, very few schools actually desegregated until Congress and the president began to push for desegregation in the mid–1960s.[11] Moreover, Donald Horowitz, as well as other scholars, raised questions about the detrimental consequences of judicial policy making, such as the unanticipated consequences of using an individual case concerning two specific litigants as the vehicle for making far-reaching policy decisions that affect many people whose circumstances may be different than those of the litigants.[12]

Although it is less well recognized by the general public, federal judges also wield significant influence over court reform and judicial administration. Just as scholars' understanding of judicial power over policy making required refinement and clarification, so, too, does knowledge about federal judges' influence over judicial administration. Because judicial policy making, with its impact on visible and controversial public policy issues, virtually captured the attention of judicial scholars, relatively few researchers focus on the role of federal judges in shaping court reform and other aspects of judicial administration.

The Federal Judicial Center, an official division of the judicial branch, produces numerous studies that examine the problems and successes of specific court reform innovations, such as court-annexed arbitration and other forms of alternative dispute resolution.[13] However, these government-sponsored projects focus on prescriptive program evaluation and do not take a critical view of judges as *political* actors who possess self-interest and undertake strategic actions as a means to advance those interests. Scholarly works that recognize the underlying political aspects of federal judges' role in judicial administration necessarily focus on particular topics and emphasize how judges influence judicial administration. For example, Peter Fish explored the history of federal judicial administration;[14] Deborah Barrow and Thomas Walker examined a specific court reform initiative, the creation of the Eleventh Circuit Court of Appeals;[15] and Malcolm Feeley studied the implementation of the federal Speedy Trial Act.[16] Much remains to be explored not only about how federal judges influence judicial administration, but also about why they adopt specific strategies and how their influence over judicial administration affects the judicial process and society at large.

In the chapters that follow, this book seeks to refine and clarify the contemporary understandings about the influence of federal judges over judicial administration. Their influence will be examined by analyzing four issues: the Judicial Improvements Act of 1990, judicial salary reform, habeas corpus reform, and the bureaucratization of federal courthouses. The goal of this study is to move beyond a discussion of how judges influence court reform in order to examine why judges are motivated to act and how their actions affect American society and the quality of justice produced by the federal courts.

The effort to examine judges' motivations as well as the consequences of judicially influenced court reform represents an attempt to link this study to broader understandings of political phenomena that affect the governing system. By examining judges' motivations, the federal judiciary can be more clearly recognized as an identifiable interest that reacts against threats to its status, autonomy, and authority. This is not to say that all federal judges are like-minded and universally share common views about issues affecting court administration. Although individual judges may disagree with each other about some issues, such disagreements are common among members of recognized interest groups. For example, dues-paying members of the American Civil Liberties Union sometimes disagree with each other about the extent to which the organization's resources should be devoted to protecting the free speech rights of Nazis and the Ku Klux Klan.[17] An interest group can be recognized and its activities analyzed when representatives of an interest take strategic actions to influence the decisions of governmental actors, whether or not every member of the group supports those actions.

If an interest group is defined as "an organized body of individuals who share some goals and who try to influence public policy,"[18] then federal judges deserve the label "interest group" when they use their resources and authority to affect court administration. Sometimes judges' strategic, self-interested actions are carried out by formal organizations such as the Judicial Conference of the United States or the Federal Judges Association. In other contexts, individual judges advance judicial self-interest by using their authority in overseeing administrative procedures in individual courthouses or making decisions in individual appellate cases. The chapters that follow provide examples of both organized, coordinated strategies and individual judges' actions as the sources of federal judges' self-interested influence over court administration.

The foregoing analytical approach for understanding judges' motivations and strategies places these authoritative judicial officers in the mainstream of political scientists' understandings about why and how political interests act strategically to achieve favorable policy outcomes. In addition, the emphasis on societal consequences of court reform enhances the recognition that "judicial policy making" should not be narrowly conceptualized as based entirely on considered judgments contained in formal judicial decisions. Instead, consistent with the scholarly literature on public policy, structural and procedural changes in authoritative institutions must be recognized as impacting not only individual policy outcomes, but also the role of authoritative institutions within the governing system and society at large. Thus when judges act to influence judicial administration, their actions can have broad consequences, especially for the processing of cases and the determination of outcomes for individual litigants and defendants.

It should be emphasized from the outset that this examination of judges' self-interest is neither a simple exposé nor a critique of the federal judiciary. The recognition of self-interest as an inherent, if not innate, element of basic human nature permeates the design of the institutions and processes of American society. The reliance of the economic system on markets and free enterprise represents an attempt to use self-interested economic decisions to promote economic growth that will benefit the entire society. The electoral processes for selecting government leaders and policy makers seek to employ the mechanism of democratic accountability to propel self-interested political decisions that will serve and benefit society. Elected representatives seek to retain their offices through reelection, and therefore, their self-interest should cause them to be sensitive and responsive to the values and policy preferences of the voters in society. Recent policy initiatives, such as providing parents with choices about which schools their children will attend, also represent efforts to use self-interested decisions by policy consumers to force beneficial reactions by education officials, who must cater to these consumers' desires in order to survive.

The underlying point of this study is to examine federal judges in light of the self-interested decision making that shapes and drives American society. Fundamentally, the question for the courts and American society is "How can we best shape and harness judges' self-interested decision making in order to advance the most broadly beneficial judicial institutions, processes, and policies?" Although this question cannot be easily answered, it can never even be explored at all without a clear recognition of the role of judges' self-interest in court administration.

JUDGES IN THE FEDERAL COURTS

The United States Constitution provides the basic description of the power and functions of federal judges. Article III in the Constitution describes judges' power by saying that "judicial Power . . . shall be vested in one supreme Court, and in such inferior Courts as the Congress may from time to time ordain and establish."[19] Subsequent sections of Article III describe the applicability of the judicial power to "all Cases, in Law and Equity, arising under this Constitution, [and] the Laws of the United States" as well as to cases involving treaties, ambassadors, citizens of different states, the U.S. government, and state governments—when they are in conflict with other states or citizens of other states.[20] In essence, the Constitution paints a picture of federal judges who have the power to act as stereotypical judicial decision makers in presiding over and deciding certain kinds of legal cases.

While the Constitution says that federal judges shall decide certain categories of cases, it has little to say about the structure and administration of the federal court system. The Constitution makes four declarations about federal judicial administration. First, there shall be one Supreme Court. Second, other federal courts shall be created by Congress as it sees fit. This provision places responsibility for the design of the judicial system in the hands of the people's elected representatives in the legislative branch. Third, federal judges shall be appointed by the president, be confirmed by the Senate, and serve "during good Behaviour," which can effectively mean life tenure. Fourth, federal judges' salaries cannot be diminished while they are in office. Taken as a whole, these provisions (i.e., life tenure and protected salaries) seek to create an independent judiciary that makes judicial decisions in a hierarchical court system (i.e., one Supreme Court and various lower levels of courts) designed and reformed by Congress.

Most of the Constitution's original blueprint for the federal judiciary is in evidence in the contemporary court system. Federal judges, who are insulated from partisan political pressures through their protected tenure and salaries, make decisions about the specific categories of cases listed in

Article III within a hierarchical judicial system containing trial courts (U.S. district courts), intermediate appellate courts (U.S. circuit courts of appeals), and one Supreme Court. The one element in the original constitutional blueprint that deviates most significantly from the framers' vision is the expectation of congressional control over the design and reform of the federal court system.

As a formal matter, it is indeed true that Congress must pass legislation to determine the structures, processes, and resources of the judicial branch of government. Upon closer examination, however, it is clear that the people's elected representatives in Congress do not simply use their own best judgment about how the federal courts should operate. Instead, federal judges exert significant, yet not always visible, influence over judicial administration.

Analysts of American politics and government from James Madison to twentieth-century political scientists have recognized that American politics and government are shaped by the strategic interactions of interests.[21] People who are motivated by shared self-interest and values can, if they possess resources and knowledge, translate those shared interests into political action aimed at moving the government to advance specific policy goals favorable to their values and self-interest. Americans are accustomed to seeing various kinds of groups with shared interests, such as political parties and organized interest groups. These groups seek to advance their goals by lobbying Congress, supporting political candidates, initiating policy-oriented litigation, and otherwise acting to push the legislative, executive, and judicial branches of government to act in their favor. Although federal judges are usually pictured as judicial decision makers who are preoccupied with legal cases and removed from the day-to-day conflicts and interactions of American politics, their role and behavior are different when they are confronted with issues that affect their status, power, and accoutrements of judicial office. Thus, a central theme of this book is that federal judges should be more clearly recognized as a self-interested group that is well positioned to shape judicial administration and court reform initiatives.

In considering the interest and power of federal judges over judicial administration, the reasons for their interest are more easily recognized than the sources and implementation of their power. The basis for judges' involvement in the structures and processes of the federal courts can best be examined by considering three underlying elements: self-interest, opportunity, and influence.

Self-Interest

Federal judges are mere human beings in black robes. Although this observation may be self-evident, it has significant implications that clash with the image of judges possessed by many segments of the public and perpetuated by the judges themselves. As Harry Stumpf observed, perpetuation of the myth of judicial neutrality suits the interests of both judges and the public:

With symbols such as law degrees, robes, walnut-paneled courtrooms, elevated benches, a special language, and the like, we help to sustain the myth of an impersonal judiciary divining decisions based on some objective truth contained in the Constitution (another symbol), and knowable only by a select few. It is all a very reassuring view of policy-making (or rather, rule divining), . . . after the tumult, greed, and indecisiveness of the legislative process. . . . Judges, for their part, are more than anxious to tout the salutary qualities of their medicament. They can hardly be faulted for packaging and marketing a product that is in such large demand by the public.[22]

Despite the prevalence of the wishful myth of formal law, the *human-ness* of judges is not difficult to discern. A significant body of judicial scholarship has demonstrated how judicial decisions stem not from "the law," but from the attitudes, values, policy preferences, and interactions of judges.[23] Because they are human beings, rather than mechanical appliers of the law, judges possess the attributes and failings of other human beings. Possession of a legal education, legal experience, and an authoritative judicial office does not cleanse judges of their attitudes and emotions. More important, judicial office does not remove the incumbents' human inclinations to identify and pursue their own self-interest.

By virtue of their office, federal judges have power, prestige, and significant autonomy as well as salaries and benefits that are better than those possessed by all but a few Americans. Like other people who seek to preserve and enhance their valued possessions, judges work to maintain and expand the beneficial aspects of judicial office. Thus, as human beings, judges have an understandable self-interest in shaping court structures and procedures in ways that preserve their powers and privileges. Their actions affecting judicial administration frequently reflect their shared self-interest.

The pursuit of self-interest by judges should not necessarily be regarded as either a manifestation of personal selfishness or inherently bad for society. Judges' actions to preserve their own authority and status may have functional benefits for the system by maintaining the effectiveness and legitimacy of the judicial branch. Indeed, judges will claim and geninuely believe that their actions are intended to benefit the court system. Even in their pursuit of salary increases, judges attempted to cast their arguments as advocacy for preserving morale and stability within the judiciary. Although these are legitimate and important goals for the federal judges to advance, there is always a risk that decision makers will fail to recognize the extent and consequences of self-interest as they advance policy objectives in the name of broad, systemic goals. The identification of self-interested motivations by judges is not intended to condemn judges for being insufficiently selfless. Instead, the purpose is to illuminate how judges' motivations and actions are comparable to those of other political interests. Moreover, the recognition of judges' self-interest provides a basis for questioning the judges' justifications for their actions and for assessing whether or not the judges recognize the consequences of their self-interested actions.

Opportunity

Federal judges' opportunity to affect and frequently even control court reform and other aspects of judicial administration stems from their independence. The Constitution grants life tenure to federal judges to ensure that they will be able to make courageous and correct decisions without fearing removal from office by partisan political interests that may oppose their decisions. Thus the federal judiciary differs significantly from the many state judicial systems that emphasize accountability instead of independence by permitting voters to select judges in periodic elections.[24]

The life tenure granted to federal judges creates the opportunity for judges to act in ways that advance their self-interest because they are not directly accountable to any higher authority. Although they can be removed from office through impeachment, that cumbersome removal mechanism is reserved only for wayward judicial officers who commit crimes or gross ethical violations. Judges who step outside of their stereotypical role as judicial decision makers face little risk of sanctions when they lobby Congress, initiate court reform experiments within their courthouses, or otherwise shape the procedures, policies, and structures of the federal courts in self-interested ways. This is not to say that judges can always do as they please and openly behave in a dictatorial fashion. On the contrary, because the judiciary is dependent on Congress for resources, judges must employ political sensibilities that will maintain their legitimacy and credibility in the eyes of legislators.

Judges' opportunity to control judicial administration is enhanced by the fundamental constitutional principle of separation of powers. Because each branch of government was given a separate sphere of authority in order to avoid the excessive accumulation of power in any single set of hands, decision makers in the legislative and executive branches of government are cognizant of the need to defer to judges about many matters concerning the judicial branch. The Constitution gives Congress the power to create and change nearly any aspect of court organization and procedure for federal courts other than the Supreme Court,[25] yet concerns about preserving separation of powers lead legislators to consult with and defer to judges when considering legislative initiatives affecting the judicial branch. Moreover, there is a very practical reason for decision makers in the legislative and executive branches to respect judges' views about separation of powers when discussing court reform: If there is ever any disagreement about whether or not a court reform statute violates the constitutional principle of separation of powers, it is the federal judges who will ultimately decide the issue when it enters the court system in the form of a legal case.

An additional element that creates opportunities for judges to control judicial administration is the fragmentation of power inherent in the federal court system. Individual judges control the conduct of litigation within their own courthouses. It can be difficult to force life-tenured judges to comply with judicial administration policies that they oppose. For example, Feeley found that "[j]udicial resistance . . . [was] the primary factor in delayed implementation" of the federal Speedy Trial Act of 1974.[26] Local lawyers may be reluctant to challenge or complain about individual judges' improper or idiosyncratic court administration procedures because the lawyers know that they will be spending the rest of their careers appearing before the judge at the local federal courthouse and they do not want to jeopardize their prospects for winning future cases.

Influence

A major source of the federal judiciary's influence over issues affecting judicial administration can be recognized by answering this question: "Who are the human beings who are selected to become federal judges?" Federal judges are not selected at random from among American lawyers. They are also not selected because they have proven themselves to possess the best legal minds. Federal judges are selected through a political process in which the president and members of Congress, especially U.S. senators, reward loyal allies from within their political parties.[27] Historically, senators have determined the selection of district judges and influenced the selection of circuit judges within their home states when their political party controlled the White House. Federal judges are usually lawyers who were active in politics or had close relationships with members of Congress and political party leaders.[28] As a result of their political backgrounds and relationships with members of Congress, federal judges have historically been able to communicate their preferences effectively to Congress, despite a formal prohibition on lobbying by federal judges.

EXAMPLE: CREATION OF THE U.S. MAGISTRATE JUDGES

Federal judges' influence over court reform was in evidence when Congress created a new judicial officer during the late 1960s. Congress created the office of U.S. magistrate in 1968 in order to replace the U.S. commissioners who, since 1793, had set bail, issued warrants, and handled petty criminal offenses. There were numerous problems with the use of the commissioners. For example, many of the commissioners had no legal training or other relevant qualifications, decisions by commissioners were often in conflict with settled law, and the commissioners were paid on a fee-per-case basis that created at least an appearance of impropriety for judicial officers.[29] The new magistrate system was designed to alleviate those flaws by requiring legal qualifications and paying set salaries while expanding the range of activities to be performed by the new judicial officers.[30] Although some members of Congress attempted to gain personal publicity and political support by portraying the magistrates as new officers for fighting crime, the history of the Magistrates Act and the language of the statute make clear that the magistrates were actually intended to be a resource for generally enhancing the effectiveness of the federal courts.[31]

Under the authorizing statute,[32] magistrates, who later had their title changed to magistrate judges, were granted the authority to undertake a wide range of tasks to assist the district courts. Magistrate judges possess a variety of powers: all powers and duties previously exercised by the commissioners, the authority to detain criminal defendants prior to trial or set bail, and the authority to undertake "such additional duties as are not inconsistent with the Constitution and laws of the United States."[33] For dispositive motions, magistrate judges may preside over hearings and submit reports of findings and recommended dispositions to a district judge for review and approval. On all other motions, magistrate judges may make determinations that are appealable to district judges. Moreover, even though magistrate judges are selected for renewable eight-year terms and therefore are not Article III judicial officers with life tenure and protected compensation, magistrate judges are authorized to conduct complete civil trials with the consent of litigants. Magistrate judges' authority is sufficiently broad that they are permitted to conduct nearly any judicial task except for trying and sentencing felons.

When Congress created the new judicial office to assist the work of the district courts, federal judges were deeply involved in planning and implementing this court reform innovation. Judges testified before congressional committees about the need for more judicial resources.[34] Congress addressed concerns about separation of powers by permitting district judges to select the lawyers who would serve as magistrates[35] and by permitting district judges to decide which tasks magistrate judges would perform within each courthouse.[36] District judges used magistrate judges according to the district judges' interests, needs, and philosophical principles. District judges who wanted to preserve their own monopoly over civil trials and other authoritative responsibilities assigned only routine tasks to their magistrate judges. By contrast, district judges who wanted to attack caseload problems aggressively and process civil cases efficiently assigned trial responsibilities to their magistrate judges. Some district judges exploited their independence and autonomy and the fragmentation of power within the federal courts to make such trial assignments *even before Congress actually amended the Magistrates Act in 1979 to permit such assignments.*[37]

Thus federal judges shaped both the design and the implementation of the new judicial office. As in other developments affecting court reform and the administration of justice, the judges' actions and influence did not attract attention because of the low public interest and low visibility of court reform issues:

Not surprisingly, the media and the public paid little attention to the reforms occurring within the federal judiciary. A review of all *New York Times* articles relevant to the Magistrates Act for the years 1965 through 1968, the years from the beginning of the first exploratory hearings through the passage and signing of the legislation, indicates that brief articles buried in the newspaper merely noted various steps in the legislative process. As with other internal judicial reforms, the planning and discussion underlying the Magistrates Act remained strictly the province of lawyers and judges.[38]

CONCLUSION

As indicated by the creation of the office of U.S. magistrate judge, federal judges' significant influence over court reform and judicial administration is often unnoticed by a disinterested public. In addition, judicial scholars are more attracted to the study of controversial judicial policy-making issues, such as abortion, affirmative action, and criminal defendants' rights. The fact that federal judges' role in judicial administration receives less attention than their role in deciding legal cases concerning public policy issues does not indicate that judicial administration is unimportant. Indeed, the structures and procedures that determine who makes decisions in the judicial process and how those decisions will be made have a significant impact on case outcomes and the quality of justice. Instead, judicial administration is a relatively neglected subject because of the inherent difficulties in gaining access to and information from a secretive branch of government. In the judiciary, authoritative officials prefer to portray an image of political detachment rather than reveal the reality of their self-interested, albeit relatively invisible, political participation in decisions that guide innovations, policies, and processes in the federal courts.

The chapters that follow examine examples of federal judges' influence over court reform and judicial administration. The discussion in Chapter 2 concerning the Judicial Improvements Act of 1990 shows how federal judicial officers, including U.S. magistrate judges, can mobilize to combat perceived threats to their status, authority, and autonomy. In Chapter 3, federal judges' blatant advancement of self-interest is revealed in the analysis of the federal judges' lobbying campaign in 1989 to gain salary increases. The examinations of habeas corpus reform in Chapter 4 and judicial bureaucracy in Chapter 5 explore the consequences of federal judges' control over judicial processes that affect case outcomes and the quality of justice. The concluding chapter discusses the implications when life-tenured officials who control one of the branches of government within a democratic governing system can influence decisions concerning judicial administration.

NOTES

1. U.S. Const., art. III § 1.
2. Brown v. Board of Education, 347 U.S. 483 (1954).
3. See, e.g., Swann v. Charlotte-Mecklenburg School District, 402 U.S. 1 (1971).
4. Mapp v. Ohio, 367 U.S. 643 (1961).
5. Engel v. Vitale, 370 U.S. 421 (1962).
6. Bounds v. Smith, 430 U.S. 817 (1977).
7. Texas v. Johnson, 491 U.S. 397 (1989).
8. Thomas G. Walker and Lee Epstein, *The Supreme Court: An Introduction* (New York: St. Martin's Press, 1993), 19.
9. Charles A. Johnson and Bradley C. Canon, *Judicial Policies: Implementation and Impact* (Washington, D.C.: Congressional Quarterly Press, 1984), 29–184.
10. Gerald Rosenberg, *The Hollow Hope: Can Courts Bring About Social Change?* (Chicago: University of Chicago Press, 1991), 46–54.
11. Ibid.
12. Donald Horowitz, *The Courts and Social Policy* (Washington, D.C.: Brookings Institution, 1977), 22–67, 255–298.
13. See, e.g., E. Allen Lind and John E. Sheppard, *Evaluation of Court-Annexed Arbitration in Three Federal District Courts* (Washington, D.C.: Federal Judicial Center, 1983); M. Daniel Jacoubovitch and Carl, M. Moore *Summary Jury Trials in the Northern District of Ohio* (Washington, D.C.: Federal Judicial Center, 1982).
14. Peter G. Fish, *The Politics of Federal Judicial Administration* (Princeton, N.J.: Princeton University Press, 1973).
15. Deborah J. Barrow and Thomas G. Walker, *A Court Divided: The Fifth Circuit Court of Appeals and the Politics of Judicial Reform* (New Haven, Conn.: Yale University Press, 1988).
16. Malcolm M. Feeley, *Court Reform on Trial* (New York: Basic Books, 1983).
17. Kay Lehman Schlozman and John T. Tierney, *Organized Interests and American Democracy* (New York: Harper & Row, 1986), 135–136.
18. Jeffrey M. Berry, *The Interest Group Society* (Boston: Little, Brown, 1984), 5.
19. U.S. Const. art. III, § 1.
20. Ibid., § 2.
21. Schlozman and Tierney, ix–13.
22. Harry P. Stumpf, *American Judicial Politics* (San Diego, Calif.: Harcourt Brace Jovanovich, 1988), 42.
23. See Jeffrey Segal and Harold Spaeth, *The Supreme Court and the Attitudinal Model* (Cambridge: Cambridge University Press, 1993); James L. Gibson, "From Simplicity to Complexity: The Development of Theory in the Study of Judicial Behavior," *Political Behavior* 5 (1983): 7–49.
24. Christopher E. Smith, *Courts, Politics, and the Judicial Process* (Chicago: Nelson-Hall, 1993), 97–105.

25. U.S. Const., art. III, § 1 ("The judicial Power of the United States, shall be vested in one supreme Court, *and in such inferior courts as the Congress may from time to time ordain and establish*" (emphasis supplied).

26. Feeley, 171.

27. Smith, *Courts, Politics, and the Judicial Process*, 110–117, 254–260.

28. See, e.g., Sheldon Goldman, "The Bush Imprint on the Judiciary: Carrying on a Tradition," *Judicature* 74 (1991): 294–306.

29. Peter G. McCabe, "The Federal Magistrates Act of 1979," *Harvard Journal on Legislation* 16 (1979): 345–347.

30. Joseph F. Spaniol, Jr., "The Federal Magistrate Act: History and Development," *Arizona State Law Journal* (1974): 566–570.

31. House Report No. 1629, Federal Magistrates Act, *U.S. Code Congressional and Administrative News* (1968): 4257.

32. 28 U.S.C. §§ 631–639.

33. 28 U.S.C. § 636(b)(3).

34. See Testimony of the Hon. Edward S. Northrup, Senate Committee on the Judiciary, *Federal Magistrates Act: Hearings Before the Subcommittee on Improvements in Judicial Machinery on S. 3475 and S. 945*, 89th Cong., 2d Sess., and 90th Cong., 1st Sess. (1966 and 1967), 52.

35. See Christopher E. Smith, "Merit Selection Committees and the Politics of Appointing United States Magistrates," *Justice System Journal* 12 (1987): 210–231.

36. See Christopher E. Smith, "Assessing the Consequences of Judicial Innovation: U.S. Magistrates' Trials and Related Tribulations," *Wake Forest Law Review* 23 (1988): 455–490.

37. Ibid., 462–466.

38. Christopher E. Smith, *United States Magistrates in the Federal Courts: Subordinate Judges* (New York: Praeger, 1990), 18.

2

Judicial Lobbying and Court Reform

The United States Constitution employs the concept of separation of powers in order to prevent the accumulation of excessive power within a single branch of government. As the Supreme Court observed in *Immigration and Naturalization Service v. Chadha*, "The Constitution sought to divide the delegated powers of the new Federal Government into three defined categories, Legislative, Executive, and Judicial, to assure, as nearly as possible, that each Branch of government would confine itself to its assigned responsibility."[1]

Because the Constitution grants to Congress the exclusive power to raise revenue and enact spending programs,[2] an inevitable consequence of the governing system's division of authority is that all of the branches of government are dependent upon the legislative branch for the allocation of resources and the creation of institutional structures and programs. In the federal system, for example, only the United States Supreme Court was established by Article III of the Constitution. Congress shapes the organization and authority of other components of the judicial branch because, according to the Constitution, lower courts are the "inferior Courts [that] the Congress may from time to time ordain and establish."[3] Thus federal judicial officers must attempt to persuade or influence Congress in order to gain sufficient resources and to ensure that court organization and procedures fulfill judicial actors' needs and expectations.

How do judicial officers attempt to influence the legislative branch? What are the consequences of judicial officers' political tactics aimed at shaping legislative actions that affect the courts? Because of the secrecy that shrouds activities "behind the purple curtain" of the judiciary, it can be difficult for outsiders to assess the nature and results of judicial lobbying. For example, interviews with judges and government officials have provided insights into federal appellate judges' strategic activities that affected the congressional decision to divide the old Fifth Circuit Court of Appeals into two circuits.[4] That study, however, has been criticized for failing to analyze judicial lobbying "in particular depth [and] with . . . attention given to problems such lobbying can entail."[5] Thus much remains to be learned about judicial officers' tactics in seeking to influence legislative enactments.

Officially, the federal judges communicate to Congress through the Judicial Conference of the United States. The Judicial Conference is the primary policy-making body for the judicial branch. The chief justice presides over the Judicial Conference, which is composed of chief judges representing each of the circuit courts plus one district judge from each circuit. The Judicial Conference makes recommendations to Congress concerning the policies, procedures, and resource needs of the judicial branch. The judges also have their own association, the Federal Judges Association, which serves as an additional vehicle through which the judges, or at least some portion of them, can communicate to Congress with a unified voice. Like other organized interests, the judges are also often able to enlist the support of other groups, such as bar associations, to provide additional communication with and pressure on Congress to enact the judicial policies recommended by the judges or to block legislation that the judges oppose. The judges do not possess the ability to set the legislative agenda, and neither of their organizations can control the decisions made by Congress. However, the existence of an official body for policy recommendations as well as an external interest group gives the judges multiple avenues for communicating their desires to politicians and the public.

In addition, appointees to Article III judgeships tend to have close connections to members of Congress and leaders within political parties:

If politics enlarges the career opportunities of American lawyers, so it restricts eligibility for high judicial office. Judgeships are normally rewards for political service. As a distinguished federal judge observed: "You can't get on the federal bench in this country without a political claim. I had a political claim, and so did every one of my colleagues."[6]

Unlike the Article III judges, who possess "well-developed relationships with one or more legislators . . . because they were active politically prior to assuming a position on the federal bench,"[7] other judicial actors do not possess such advantages for lobbying legislators.

The U.S. magistrate judges, for example, receive their appointments as subordinate judicial officers from district judges rather than from connections to political parties, members of Congress, and the president. Full-time magistrates are appointed to eight-year renewable terms in office by the district judges for whom they will work. Because the office of magistrate judge has evolved rapidly during the two decades since its creation and because magistrate judges' precise roles were not clearly defined by Congress, these subordinate judicial officers have been keenly interested in encouraging legislative developments that will enhance their status and authority within the federal courts. For example, the magistrates have their own national association, the Federal Magistrate Judges Association, which works to improve the status, authority, salary, and benefits of the federal courts' subordinate judicial officers. Prior to 1991, the Association was called the National Council of U.S. Magistrates. The Association engaged in typical "interest group" behavior by keeping its membership informed about issues and by attempting to influence the Judicial Conference of the United States and Congress on behalf of the magistrates. Even magistrates who are not active in the Association display a strong interest in protecting and expanding their status and authority: "Although not all magistrates agree that judicial officers should act as an interest group and many magistrates do not participate in the national organization, the magistrates generally manifest many characteristics of any occupational interest group that undertakes planned, political actions on behalf of the group's collective interests."[8]

In discussing the role of the federal judiciary in shaping legislation affecting judicial administration, this chapter will focus on the development and consequences of the Judicial Improvements Act of 1990. Although this legislation concerned broad court reform issues, such as the implementation of alternative dispute resolution and differentiated case management programs, one element of the legislation illustrates the activation and successful pursuit of self-interest by the federal judges. When federal judges saw their autonomy threatened by court reform proposals, they reacted by becoming involved in shaping legislation that ultimately preserved their control over the judicial process. Simultaneously, U.S. magistrate judges, the subordinate judicial officers who work with and for district judges, reacted to legislative proposals that would have curtailed their status and authority within the judicial branch. Because the magistrate judges sought and gained a title change from "U.S. magistrates" to "U.S. magistrate judges," the discussion in subsequent sections of this chapter will refer to these officials as "magistrates" in explaining their goals and status prior to their successful lobbying effort.

Although the judges succeeded in preserving their autonomy in this legislative battle, they do not always achieve their goals. In particular, they cannot readily make a Congress which is distracted by a plethora of pressing issues pay attention to judicial matters. As this case study illustrates, however, when Congress moves forward with legislative activity that affects the judiciary, the judges have significant abilities to shape even those court administration enactments that they cannot control.

JUDICIAL LOBBYING

Judges obviously have a special interest in court reform legislation. Because judges supervise the administration of the judicial process, they have good reason to be concerned about how reform legislation will affect the courts. For example, when Congress considered legislation during the 1970s to require "speedy trials" in criminal cases, judges evinced strong concerns about how the proposed reforms would affect both the administration of justice and the judges' traditional authority over the judicial branch: "Judges complained that the bill's planning provisions encroached upon their management prerogatives, and that requiring prosecutors, clerks, and other nonjudicial members of the criminal justice system to take part in planning violated separation of powers."[9]

Judges not only have a strong interest in court reform legislation, but also can have tremendous influence over the development and success of court reform initiatives. This influence can take two forms. First, legislators can defer to the judges' expertise about the needs of judicial administration in making some policy decisions. For example, judges played an influential role in the decision to divide the old Fifth Circuit U.S. Court of Appeals into a smaller Fifth Circuit (including Texas, Louisiana, and Mississippi) and a new Eleventh Circuit (including Alabama, Georgia, and Florida):

[T]he large Fifth Circuit was overloaded with cases and needed to be split into two new circuits. This . . . was extremely controversial, because civil rights supporters feared that splitting the Fifth Circuit and adding new judges would dilute important civil rights gains made during the 1950s and 1960s. Congress took no early action. But, with all of the judges in the Fifth Circuit supporting the split, Congress complied in 1980.[10]

Second, judges can use their autonomy in controlling the administration of individual courthouses to shape, or even thwart, legislated court reform initiatives. If legislators attempt to impose new procedures with which judges disagree, because of the fragmentation of power within the judicial system, individual judges may hinder the implementation of new practices within their courthouses. For example, as Malcolm Feeley found in his study of criminal justice reforms, judges thwarted efforts to reform bail and sentencing policies in the criminal justice system: "A great many judges quite simply do not regard liberalized pretrial release or mandatory sentences as desirable and [thus the judges] thwart [the new policies'] implementation."[11] Such judicial influence over the effects of legislative enactments is an inevitable result of the autonomy and discretionary authority necessarily vested in judges.

Although judges influence court reform initiatives that emanate from Congress, they do not automatically control Congress's actions. Legislators may reflexively defer to judges on some issues, but they may not defer to judges on other issues when they or their constituents strongly desire a specific change in law, legal procedures, or judicial organization. Thus when judicial officers seek to initiate or to influence the formulation of legislation on some issues, the judges' dependence upon legislative action forces them to engage in the kinds of political strategies, such as lobbying and persuasion, that other interested parties employ when seeking beneficial legislation.

When judicial officers seek to influence the content of court reform legislation, they are governed by the legal and ethical rules that constrain judges' behavior. Under federal law, judges may not attempt to influence Congress by using public funds. The statutory language limiting the judges' activities is quite specific:

No part of money appropriated by any enactment of Congress, shall, in the absence of express authorization by Congress be used directly or indirectly to pay for any personal service, advertisement, telegram, telephone, letter, printed or written matter, or other device, intended to influence in any manner a Member of Congress, to favor or oppose, by vote or otherwise, any legislation or appropriation by Congress. . . .[12]

In addition, according to the ethical proscriptions directed at judges in the American Bar Association's Code of Judicial Conduct, judges may testify before and consult with other branches of government, "but only on matters concerning the administration of justice."[13] Federal law mirrors this invitation for limited communications between judges and legislators by declaring that the prohibition on the use of public funds for lobbying "shall not prevent officers . . . of the United States . . . from communicating to Members of Congress, through proper official channels, requests for legislation or appropriations which they deem necessary for the efficient conduct of the public business."[14]

Although there are opportunities for limited interbranch communications, the concerns about the impropriety of judicial lobbying lead judges to act cautiously when communicating with Congress. Judge Frank Coffin, for example, believes that formal prohibitions on judicial lobbying have detrimentally inhibited necessary communications between the branches of government:

The essence of the problem can be summed up by saying that the overarching and simplistic commandment, "thou shalt not lobby," does not begin to recognize the multiple levels and purposes of desirable communication in both directions between the two great branches. Worse, the negative nature of the commandment and its criminal sanction chill any effort to explore ways of meeting perceived needs.[15]

Scholars have echoed Judge Coffin's position that communications between judges and Congress are not merely beneficial, but are indeed essential:

The idea of judicial lobbying is anathema to many. It somehow seems inappropriate for federal judges, whose adjudicative role requires neutrality rather than advocacy, to urge the passage or defeat of proposed legislation. In spite of its negative connotations, however, lobbying is nothing more than communicating information and considered opinion to the appropriate decisionmakers. No one has more accurate information on matters of judicial administration or is in a better position to comment on conditions facing the courts than the federal judge. . . . It is both proper and essential for this communication process to function effectively.[16]

Despite the concerns that useful interbranch communications are hindered, the U.S. attorney general has actually interpreted the statutory prohibition on lobbying by judges relatively loosely. The attorney general's interpretation permits relevant communications between judges and members of Congress without narrowly construing the requirement that such communications pass through "official channels."[17]

Although there are no strenuously enforced, precise regulations on judicial lobbying, judges must be concerned about the propriety of their behavior in expressing their views about legislation. As characterized in one study: "[J]udicial lobbying must occur under certain restraints and limitations. Mindful of the proper judicial role, judges cannot roam the corridors of Congress buttonholing members and pleading the case of the courts."[18] Thus federal judges must act carefully when they lay the groundwork for effective strategic communications with Congress concerning the administration of the federal courts. As one subtle strategy, for example, the Budget Committee of the Judicial Conference of the United States seeks to enhance its influence with Congress by being comprised of judges "having ability, legislative experience, and congressional associations."[19] By exploiting preexisting relationships between judges who were appointed through the political process and the members of Congress who helped to have them appointed, the judiciary can presumably improve the efficacy of the communications that it initiates with the legislative branch about matters of self-interest, such as the judicial budget and court reform.

THE ROLE OF THE JUDICIAL CONFERENCE
AND THE CHIEF JUSTICE

Because judicial officers cannot behave like other lobbyists who prowl the corridors of Congress and donate money to political campaigns, "articulating the views of the courts normally occurs through well-established, institutionalized channels."[20] Thus the Judicial Conference of the United States serves as the legislative liaison between the federal judiciary and Congress.[21] The Judicial Conference is "[t]he central administrative policymaking organization of the federal judicial system. . . .—composed of the chief justice of the Supreme Court as the presiding member, the chief judges of each of the judicial circuits, one district judge from each of the twelve regional circuits, and the chief judge of the court of international trade."[22] Although there have been criticisms of the Judicial Conference's effectiveness in persuading Congress about the needs of the judiciary,[23] Congress often defers to judges or seeks the Judicial Conference's endorsement when considering court reform legislation. For example, "[v]irtually all major legislation affecting the [Supreme] Court's jurisdiction was drafted by justices and was the result of their lobbying."[24]

Chief justices who are keenly interested in court administration can use the Judicial Conference's position and resources to educate and influence Congress. The creation of the Judicial Conference itself as well as the Administrative Office of the U.S. Courts is attributable to the effective lobbying efforts of a chief justice, William Howard Taft: "[T]he leadership of Chief Justice Taft is usually said to have been the most immediate catalyst for administrative reform [of the federal courts]. He, more than any other single individual, was responsible for persuading Congress to have a new look at the organization of the federal judiciary."[25] As described by Robert Steamer:

[Chief Justice Taft] loved being a judge and making difficult choices in hard controversies, but he was also a politician, a mover and shaker, and he held tenaciously to the view that his office called for leadership across a broad spectrum of activities, and he did not hesitate to use his prestige, his influence and his powers to achieve a more efficient judicial system. Always Taft remembered that successful lobbying requires strong personal involvement, attending committee hearings and keeping in touch with sympathetic souls in high places who could wield influence over others.[26]

According to scholars who study the judiciary, "[c]hief justices have a number of . . . ways of co-opting congressmen and mobilizing support."[27] A chief justice can "se[t] the issue agenda and provid[e] information" for Congress.[28] Former Chief Justice Warren Burger, in particular, used his leadership position on the Judicial Conference as a means to influence Congress on behalf of the judiciary:

After [Chief Justice William Howard] Taft, Burger was the most active in lobbying Congress and getting the assistance of the ABA in promoting his proposals. Beginning in 1978, Burger, his administrative assistant, and the directors of the Administrative Office [of the U.S. Courts] and the Federal Judicial Center met with the attorney general and representatives of the Department of Justice, as well as members of the House and Senate Judiciary Committees . . . at a "Seminar on Judicial Administration" sponsored by the Brookings Institution. The occasion allowed Burger and his staff to press for legislative changes. By delegating more of the congressional liaison work to his administrative assistant and the legislative affairs office, Burger was able to pursue a broad range of projects and devote his own time to "hardsell" luncheons and to more personal appeals to pivotal congressmen and presidential advisers.[29]

Chief Justice Burger's persistence paid dividends for the judiciary's efforts to influence court reform legislation.

Because the chief justice, as the formal head of the Judicial Conference, does not possess the exclusive authority to communicate with Congress on behalf of the federal judiciary, there are opportunities for other communications emanating from the judges that may give Congress "mixed signals." In one example, Chief Justice William Rehnquist received an unusual public rebuke from a majority of the judges on the Judicial Conference for submitting recommendations to Congress for streamlining death penalty appeals without first obtaining the approval of the other judges on the Judicial Conference.[30] The judges sent a letter to the Senate Judiciary Committee to disassociate themselves and the Judicial Conference from the proposal submitted to Congress by Chief Justice Rehnquist.[31] On other occasions, "[j]udges and judicial employees who have lost or fear the loss of their cause in the Conference arena continue to carry their case to Congress without Conference authorization."[32]

Judicial officers' strategies for communicating with Congress may not be limited to direct advice and lobbying. When federal judges sought to have their salaries raised in 1989, for example, the Judicial Conference authorized Chief Justice Rehnquist to hold an unprecedented press conference at the Supreme Court in order to publicize "the most serious threat to the future of the Judiciary and its continued operations that [the judges] have observed."[33] Such hyperbole directed at the public may diminish the judiciary's credibility when judges seek to persuade Congress that some other problem also requires immediate legislative attention. Moreover, by appealing for the public's assistance in pushing Congress to act, legislators may believe that the judges have stepped beyond the proper established framework for direct interbranch communications. Thus there may be a risk that Congress will become less receptive to further requests and suggestions from the judiciary.

Although judicial lobbying is a recurring aspect of the relationship between Congress and the federal judiciary, such activities are not without their risks. Fundamentally, because of widespread perceptions that judicial lobbying clashes with the traditional image of proper judicial behavior, strategic political activity by judges aimed at influencing legislation "may [negatively] influence popular respect for, and confidence in, courts."[34] There is also the potential for confusion and conflict when judicial officers pursue contradictory legislative goals or deviate from the established lines of communication between the Judicial Conference and Congress. Because the magistrate judges' interests have diverged from those of many Article III federal judges, their legislative goals and lobbying activities have sometimes generated opposition from other actors within the federal judiciary.

THE ORIGINS OF THE JUDICIAL IMPROVEMENTS ACT

In the late 1980s, Senator Joseph Biden, the chairman of the Senate Judiciary Committee, actively joined the policy trend toward advocating court reform legislation that would reduce the costs and delays that plague the growing litigation caseloads within the federal courts. Because there is a perception that the United States is burdened by too much litigation, which serves to increase the costs of legal services, medical insurance premiums, and general expenses for business operations, there have been many legislative proposals to place caps on civil damage awards, encourage alternative dispute resolution, and otherwise reduce costs and delays in litigation. During the early 1990s, for example, the Bush administration proposed a limit on discovery and punitive damages as well as other reforms intended to reduce the costs of litigation and the number of cases clogging the courts.[35] In order to identify specific desirable reforms for Congress to consider and to place court reform on the legislative agenda, Senator Biden asked the respected Brookings Institution to undertake a study of civil litigation in the federal courts.

Senator Biden then used the Brookings Institution Task Force's recommendations as the basis for proposed legislation to reduce costs and delays in federal civil litigation. The recommendation concerning the U.S. magistrates directly threatened the subordinate judicial officers' aspirations for greater status and authority: "Procedural Recommendation 11: Ensure in each district's plan that magistrates do not perform tasks best performed by the judiciary."[36] This recommendation presented an ominous threat to the interests of both district judges and magistrates. With respect to district judges, the provision implied that the Article III judges would be required to undertake personal supervision of tasks that, in many district courts, were delegated to the magistrates. If enacted into law, this recommendation could have reduced the autonomy and discretionary authority enjoyed by district judges in deciding which matters to assign to magistrates and law clerks and which matters to handle themselves.

With respect to the magistrates, the recommendation threatened both of their primary goals—namely, increasing their status and the breadth of their authority. The Brookings Institution Task Force's statement that magistrates should be prevented from undertaking "tasks best performed by the judiciary" strongly implied that district judges, rather than magistrates, should preside over civil trials. Thus, if embodied in legislation, the magistrates' aspirations for broad authority, and especially the authority and opportunity to preside over civil trials, could be jeopardized. Moreover, the reference to "the judiciary" as an entity separate from the magistrates implied that magistrates were not genuine, authoritative officials who deserve the status of judicial decision makers within the federal courts. This characterization clashed with magistrates' views of themselves and with their practical role as judicial officials who possess the authority to undertake virtually the same tasks as district judges, except for presiding over felony criminal trials. As one magistrate said in a speech at a conference for U.S. magistrates in 1987, " 'If we are not judicial officers, then I don't know who is.' "[37]

In January of 1990, Senator Biden submitted to Congress a bill entitled the Civil Justice Reform Act of 1990,[38] which embodied the recommendations of the Brookings Institution Task Force. Biden's bill contained several proposals to limit the permissible range of authoritative tasks to be undertaken by magistrates. One provision contained "[a] requirement that . . . a mandatory discovery–case management conference, presided over by a judge and not a magistrate, be held in all cases within 45 days following the first responsive pleading."[39] This legislative proposal represented a direct attack on the autonomy and discretionary authority of district judges. If enacted into law, this statute would have required district judges to meet with the parties in *every civil case*, a burdensome responsibility that many judges would rather delegate to subordinates or defer to some later point in the civil litigation process.

From the magistrates' perspective, the net effect of this provision would be not only to prevent them from overseeing an important step in the civil litigation process (i.e., case management conferences), but also to involve district judges more intimately in every civil case and thereby diminish the likelihood that magistrates would assume complete control over any civil cases.

Another provision of the bill would have had similar detrimental effects on the district judges' autonomy and the magistrates' goal of expanding their authoritative responsibilities: "[F]or cases assigned to the track designated for complex litigation, calendar a series of monitoring conferences, presided over by a judge and not a magistrate, for the purpose of extending stipulations, refining the formulation of issues and focusing and pacing discovery."[40] This proposed provision explicitly sought to diminish magistrates' authority over and participation in key phases of civil litigation. Thus, if judges were required to participate in scheduling conferences and to monitor the course of discovery, there would be little incentive for the litigants to consent later to have the trial heard by a "stranger" to the case—namely, a magistrate. Moreover, the district judges would be burdened by a series of tasks that they otherwise could have delegated to magistrates.

Senator Biden compounded his threat against the magistrates' aspirations by using his statement introducing the legislation to denigrate their potential independence and effectiveness as judicial officers:

The [pretrial] conference may lose some of its significance in the minds of the attorneys if presided over by a magistrate, since the unfortunate fact is that many attorneys seem to be far more willing to take frivolous positions before a magistrate. . . . [M]agistrates may themselves be more reluctant than judges to frame the contours of litigation, limit discovery, establish a date certain briefing schedule and address the full panoply of discovery–case management conference issues.[41]

Whether or not Senator Biden's comments accurately described specific magistrates in some districts, magistrates generally regard themselves as full-fledged judicial officers and do not hesitate to assert their authority over attorneys.[42]

THE GOALS OF U.S. MAGISTRATE JUDGES

The proposed Civil Justice Reform Act embodied a significant effort to reform the federal courts. The legislation had a variety of goals, including the effort to develop procedures to process civil cases quickly and without the substantial costs of drawn-out litigation. United States magistrate judges did not participate in the initiation of this reform effort. However, because the legislation would affect their status, authority, and working lives, they became deeply interested in the options considered by Congress for reforming the federal courts. Like other political interest groups involved in court reform, including the Article III judges, magistrate judges took action to influence legislative process on the basis of their assessment of how the court reform statute would affect their power and autonomy.

As described in Chapter 1, U.S. magistrate judges are important, but relatively invisible, authoritative decision makers within the federal district courts. Although Congress periodically expanded the formal authority of U.S. magistrate judges by amending the original Magistrates Act of 1968 in both 1976 and 1979, "the magistrates confront an uphill battle to assert their professional autonomy."[43] Because district judges within each courthouse control the number and types of tasks assigned to magistrates, not all magistrates enjoy opportunities to exercise the complete range of their statutory authority.

A study of the magistrates sponsored by the Federal Judicial Center (FJC) found that they could be divided into three general roles within the various district courts: "Additional Judge," overseeing a docket of complete civil cases; "Team Player," handling preliminary stages of civil and criminal cases; and "Specialist," processing specific categories of cases, primarily from prisoners and Social Security disability claimants.[44] Differences in magistrates' roles within different courthouses stemmed from judges' divergent conceptions of the appropriate tasks to be performed by a subordinate judicial officer as well as other factors, such as the composition of each district's caseload, the communication between judges and magistrates within each district, and judges' knowledge about how magistrates are utilized in other districts.[45]

Magistrates cannot control the definition of their status and authority as judicial officers. Their roles within the courts are primarily determined by their supervising district judges:

The judges of the district court directly control the range of duties and responsibilities of the magistrates whom they appoint, as well as the procedures to be followed by the magistrates. Except for certain duties formerly handled by United States commissioners under direct authority of a statute or federal rule, all jurisdiction exercised by a United States magistrate must be specifically delegated to him by a district judge or court. This relationship was clearly summarized during Senate hearings on the 1968 Act. . . .[46]

Because they were acutely aware that colleagues in some districts enjoy high status and broad authority, the magistrates formed a professional association, originally called the National Council of U.S. Magistrates, to advance collectively their shared goal of expanding their role and importance within the federal courts. In 1988, 86 percent of the 292 full-time magistrates were members of the Council, and 60 percent of the 169 part-time magistrates were members.[47] Individual magistrates often have little hope of changing the role conceptions held by the district judges for whom they work. Magistrates may gain status and authority through communication with judges and through judicial performance that increases the district judges' familiarity with the personal qualities and skills of the magistrates. However, the ability of magistrates to prove themselves to judges is limited because "[t]he contact and communication between [individual] magistrates and judges are affected by the different levels of status and authority possessed by the two judicial officers."[48] When joined with other magistrates under the auspices of a national organization, however, the magistrates can seek beneficial actions by Congress or by the Judicial Conference that will encourage district judges to recognize the magistrates as genuine federal judicial officers and to delegate to magistrates the complete range of authoritative tasks that the Magistrates Act permits these subordinate judges to perform.

One primary goal of the magistrates' National Council was to improve the salary and benefits of magistrates. The National Council expended funds to secure the services of a professional lobbyist to assist their efforts to gain greater material benefits.[49] They succeeded in gaining congressional action to upgrade their benefits and peg their salary at 92 percent of district judges' salaries.[50] Subsequently, during the Article III judges' successful campaign to gain a salary increase in 1989,[51] the judges included the magistrates' "need" for a salary increase among their arguments to Congress about the importance of increasing compensation for federal judicial officers.

[Magistrates] contribute significantly to the administration of justice in the United States and are an integral part of the Federal judicial system. When their ranks suffer the debilitating effects of inadequate compensation—in terms of ebbing morale, premature departures and recruitment difficulties—the Judiciary as a whole suffers as well.[52]

As illustrated by the salary issue, when the magistrates succeeded in linking their interests with those of the Article III judges, they benefitted from the judges' influence with Congress. By contrast, when the magistrates' goals clashed with those of the Article III judges, it was much more difficult for the magistrates to succeed in influencing Congress.

On two particular issues, the definition of magistrates' status and the effectuation of their broad statutory authority, the goals of these judicial subordinates have been at odds with those of many district judges. Many district judges want to maintain the magistrate judges in a role as clearly defined subordinates. The primary impediment to greater status and authority for magistrate judges is "resistance from judges who were reluctant to give up what had been within their exclusive authority."[53] With respect to the goals of increased status and authority, the magistrates have faced their greatest difficulties in seeking to improve their position within the federal judiciary.

In seeking to influence Congress and the Judicial Conference, the magistrates have been forced to overcome or to bypass the district judges who oppose them. Without the unified support of the influential Article III judges, it is much more difficult for the magistrates to be effective in their judicial lobbying. When seeking to lobby Congress, magistrates possess the same disadvantages as other judicial officers because of their inability to contribute to the legislators' primary goal—namely, reelection—through campaign contributions and other tactics available to nonjudicial lobbyists.[54] Moreover, the magistrates also lack the political connections that Article III judges possess from their preappointment partisan activities, which led to their positions on the federal bench. Because the magistrates are appointed by the district judges through a "merit selection" process that is controlled by the Article III district judges,[55] they lack the Article III judges' personal relationships with party leaders and members of Congress.

Magistrates' concerns about their proper status within the federal courts focused upon their dissatisfaction with their title. Many magistrates viewed the title "Judge" as a functional necessity for effective performance when presiding over trials, evidentiary hearings, settlement conferences, and other contexts in which judicial officers need to assert their official authority:

The magistrates recognize the value of high status. The title "Judge" creates a clear image in the minds of lawyers and parties about expected deference and appropriate formal behavior in the presence of an identifiable judicial officer. Magistrates have, in effect, a more authoritative voice when ruling on motions, guiding settlement negotiations, and undertaking other judicial tasks within their authority as federal judicial officers.[56]

The initial decision by Congress to call the newly created judicial officers "Magistrates" caused serious problems in some states. Although "magistrate" is a generic term for judicial officer and is a respected title in the British legal system, its use in the American federal courts "invites comparisons to odious experiences with 'magistrates' and justices of the peace in judicial systems of some states."[57] Because several states use "magistrate" as the title for low-level judicial officers, many attorneys who are unfamiliar with the federal courts erroneously believe that U.S. magistrates are also lay judges who possess only narrow authority over minor matters.

Magistrates in some districts have always been addressed as "Judge [X]" because the district judges in those courts endorsed their subordinates as full-fledged federal judicial officers and insisted that attorneys give magistrates the complete measure of respect that any federal judicial officer is entitled to receive.[58] By contrast, district judges in other courts insisted that magistrates *not* be addressed as "Judge" because they wanted to distinguish themselves from their judicial subordinates. Thus "these judges have instructed staff members to ensure that magistrates are never addressed as 'judge.' "[59] Although the magistrates' National Council and magistrates within specific circuits and districts sought to encourage an official change in title, with "Associate Judge" the most frequently mentioned alternative, officials at the Administrative Office of the U.S. Courts attempted to downplay the title controversy for fear that certain district judges would become antagonized and thereby oppose other aspects of magistrates' status and authority:

One official at the Administrative Office, a strong supporter of broad authority for magistrates, made the difficulties of this issue quite clear when, upon being told that magistrates in at least one district answer their telephones with the words "Judge [X]'s office," [he] visibly cringed and expressed the hope that certain district judges would not learn of this practice.[60]

The magistrates in one circuit voted to recommend to the Judicial Conference that U.S. magistrates henceforth be known as "Associate Judges." Because many Article III judges vigorously opposed any title change that might reduce the differentiation between district judges and magistrates and, moreover, because the magistrates also sought other goals related to pay and benefits, leaders of their National Council persuaded the circuit group to rescind the resolution. Instead, the national magistrate leaders attempted to utilize less formal means to improve the status of magistrates, such as having friendly district and circuit judges attempt to persuade the chief justice of the United States to issue an internal memorandum to the federal judiciary permitting the use of the title "Judge" for magistrates.

According to some magistrates, former Chief Justice Burger insisted on the title "Magistrate," but they hoped, in vain, that Chief Justice Rehnquist would be more supportive of their aspirations for the title "Judge."[61]

In addition to the controversy over the appropriate title for their judicial office, magistrates in several districts sought other attributes of status that are accorded to their colleagues elsewhere. For example, magistrates in a few districts were not permitted to wear the traditional black robe that indicates to attorneys and litigants that they are indeed authoritative judicial officers.[62] Petty actions by judges in several districts heightened the magistrates' desire to gain greater status through actions by Congress or the Judicial Conference:

An official at the Administrative Office stated that the biggest continuing problem within the magistrate system involves those districts in which judges will not permit the magistrates to park in the courthouse parking lot, eat in the judges' lunchroom, or do other things which, although sometimes minor in a practical sense, embody a significant symbolic message about an individual's status within a courthouse.[63]

Magistrates also sought to gain the full authority granted to them by Congress in the Magistrates Act. In particular, magistrates wanted to supervise complete civil trials with the consent of litigants. However, many district judges believed that judicial subordinates should not have such broad authority. As indicated by the foregoing discussion of magistrates' concerns about status, many district judges were unwilling to acknowledge that magistrates are authoritative judicial officers. Thus magistrates in many districts were assigned only a limited range of tasks by their supervising judges. Because Congress placed magistrates under the control of district judges in order to avoid constitutional concerns about excessive judicial authority granted to non–Article III officials, the magistrates sought to have the Judicial Conference and the chief justice encourage district judges to use magistrates to the full extent of their statutory authority.

JUDICIAL OFFICERS' ACTIONS IN THE
LEGISLATIVE PROCESS

Within days after the introduction of Senator Biden's bill in Congress, the National Council of U.S. Magistrates leaped into action to consider tactics for counteracting the undesirable aspects of the proposed legislation. As indicated by a letter sent by one National Council officer to all of the leaders within the organization, the magistrates quickly identified potential lobbying strategies and useful allies:

Should we take an activist or passivist role? If we ignore [the Brookings Institution Task Force report], might it go away? Should we rely on others, such as the

Magistrates Division [of the Administrative Office] and the Judicial Conference to protect our interests?

Should we send an immediate response to the Task Force? . . . As our members find out about the report, we must be prepared to tell them what the Council is doing about it and why.

. . . [O]ne of the first things we should do is find out as many details as we can about the proposed legislation. Here we should call on [the lobbyist we employed to work for us previously to gain better benefits]. . . .

I suggest we should attempt to marshal as much support as we can. Possibly we should contact the Federal Judges Association and coordinate with them. . . . Our most persuasive support would appear to be the trial bar. If there are other bar association groups like the Iowa State Bar which would openly support us, that should be very helpful. If [we] can obtain support from the ABA, that should be helpful too.

I am concerned about relying on support from the Judicial Conference since we have been told that Senator Biden plans fast action on the bill. The Judicial Conference is generally slow to react.[64]

As indicated by the letter, because the magistrates themselves have only a limited ability to lobby Congress effectively, they attempted to identify potential allies who could influence legislators on their behalf. Article III judges, who "carried the ball" for the magistrates when successfully obtaining increased judicial salaries, and private attorneys, who have the ability to apply traditional political pressure to elected officials through their campaign contributions and their votes, stood out as potential allies who might have the greatest influence over Congress. Interestingly, the magistrates indicated skepticism about the effectiveness of the institutionalized channel for communicating with Congress—namely the Judicial Conference—and therefore immediately considered their other strategic options for protecting their interests against threatening legislative proposals. The leaders of the National Council also acknowledged in the letter that they had to prepare to keep their constituents (i.e., the magistrates nationwide) informed and involved as lobbying strategies developed.

When faced with the threat from Senator Biden's proposed legislation, the magistrates benefitted from a convergence of their interests with those of the Article III judges. Senator Biden's bill not only proposed limiting magistrates' participation in certain pretrial conferences, but also simultaneously attempted to *require* that district judges follow a particular case management procedure. Senator Biden sought to require district judges to preside over certain pretrial conferences. Thus district judges were motivated to oppose the bill because it would interfere with their autonomy and authority in the management of litigation rather than because it would limit the authority of magistrates.

Fortunately for the magistrates, the timing of the Brookings Institution Task Force report and the Biden legislative proposal coincided with countervailing developments aimed at pressuring Congress to expand the magistrates' status and authority. In 1989, the Magistrates Division of the Administrative Office of the U.S. Courts and the Magistrates Committee of the Judicial Conference issued a joint report recommending, among other things, that the magistrates' title be changed and that litigants be given more encouragement to consent to have civil trials supervised by magistrates.[65] In a manner analogous to the executive branch agencies that, according to traditional political science literature, are "captured" by the interest groups that they supposedly supervise and regulate,[66] the Magistrates Division serves as a supportive advocate for the aspirations of the magistrates. For example:

During a Federal Judicial Center training conference for magistrates from several circuits, it was apparent that magistrates exhibit many of the characteristics one would expect from any interest group. Virtually all of the magistrates scheduled to address the conference on relevant developments in case law devoted significant portions of their speeches to discussion of status, salary, and pension issues affecting magistrates. These talks were so explicitly addressed to magistrates as a group that they even included reports on lobbying expenditures and political activities by the magistrates' national association. Throughout these digressions, as well as in other portions of the conference, it was apparent that the representatives of the Federal Judicial Center and the Administrative Office were "captured" bureaucrats who support the goals and aspirations of the interest group that they are responsible for managing.[67]

The actions of the officials in the Magistrates Division in openly endorsing the magistrates' aspirations were well timed to support arguments against Senator Biden's legislative initiatives.

In addition, Chief Justice Rehnquist appointed a "blue ribbon committee" in 1989 comprised of federal judges and lawyers that examined practices and procedures in the federal courts in order to consider potentially beneficial court reforms. Although this committee studied many of the same issues as the Brookings Institution Task Force, it was completely separate from the Brookings study initiated by Senator Biden. The 36-member Brookings Institution Task Force was composed of law professors and lawyers from various law firms, corporations, and public interest groups. One member of the task force was a former federal judge (Shirley Hufstedler), and another was the former director of the Federal Judicial Center (Leo Levin). By contrast, the Federal Courts Study Committee's membership was dominated by people who were much more closely connected to the federal judiciary and to relevant decision makers in Congress. The 15-member committee included five federal judges, two members of the Senate Judiciary Committee, two members of the House Judiciary Committee, a former Solicitor General of the United States, a state supreme court justice, and several lawyers.

The Federal Courts Study Committee's 1990 report made recommenda-tions that contradicted those made by the Brookings Institution Task Force by advocating that "Congress . . . allow district judges and magistrates to remind the parties [in civil litigation] of the possibilities of consent to civil trials before magistrates."[68] In effect, the committee recommended a statu-tory change that would support magistrates' aspirations for broader authority by encouraging the creation of more opportunities for magis-trates to preside over complete civil trials. By supporting the magistrates' aspirations, the recommendation also endorsed the continuation and ex-pansion of district judges' autonomy and discretionary authority to refer all aspects of civil litigation to magistrates. The Federal Courts Study Committee's report provided a strong alternative to the Brookings Insti-tution Task Force's recommendations as the basis for congressional action on court reform legislation. Moreover, the committee's report emanated from the federal judiciary and from influential members of the congres-sional judiciary committees, so that it effectively carried endorsements from important segments of both relevant branches of government. There-fore, unlike the Brookings Institution Task Force's recommendations, the report did not come from commentators and critics outside of the legisla-tive process.

Prominent district judges testified in opposition to Senator Biden's bill by arguing that limitations on magistrates' tasks and authority would hamper the proposed legislation's underlying purpose of improving case-processing efficiency. The judges argued that Senator Biden's bill would create the need for many more new Article III judges, a prospect that was potentially expensive as well as politically difficult at a moment in history when different political parties controlled the White House and Congress. According to Judge Aubrey Robinson, chief judge of the District of Colum-bia: "[T]he proposed diminution of the role of magistrates would reverse improvements made in civil case management through the increased use of magistrates, and would result in a vastly greater need for more life-ten-ured judges."[69] District judges also refuted Senator Biden's assertions that implied that magistrates were not as sufficiently independent and powerful as judicial officers to control the course of civil litigation. Judge Richard Enslen from the Western District of Michigan testified:

[Magistrates] have informed me that it is a rare occasion indeed, that any attorney ever takes a frivolous position when appearing before them. If that should occur in some districts, I suspect that it is more of a reflection of how the magistrates are perceived by the Article III judges, and what duties or powers those judges have permitted the magistrates to perform. If that suspicion be true, one way to address the concerns of the [Brookings Institution] Task Force is to leave the matter of who presides at the conference to the discretion of the district court adopting its plan.[70]

Although the National Council of U.S. Magistrates feared that the Judicial Conference would react too slowly to influence Congress concerning the proposed legislation, in fact, the Judicial Conference acted swiftly at its March 1990 meeting by voting to oppose Senator Biden's bill.[71] Thus the federal judiciary was united in opposition to the legislation, and, as indicated by studies of judicial lobbying, Congress is especially receptive to communications from judicial officers when the judges appear to speak with a unified voice.[72] The Senate Judiciary Committee scrapped Biden's proposal and proceeded to work with the federal judiciary to develop alternative court reform legislation. As a result, Congress eventually passed the Judicial Improvements Act of 1990[73] instead of Senator Biden's version of the Civil Justice Reform bill.

Although the judicial lobbying effort was ultimately successful in derailing Biden's proposals and replacing them with the judiciary's desired alternatives, the judges' tactics during the formulation of the legislation irritated members of the Senate Judiciary Committee because it appeared that the judges' viewpoints and priorities changed abruptly as the legislation was being shaped to suit the judiciary. In particular, the members of the Senate Judiciary Committee believed that a specific four-member task force of federal judges appointed by Chief Justice Rehnquist contained the spokespersons for the judiciary. After working closely with the judges on the task force, the senators were annoyed when the Judicial Conference subsequently voiced formal opposition to Senator Biden's revised legislative proposals and pushed the legislators to make further alterations in the court reform bill.

The Senate Judiciary Committee's report on the legislation described the "[n]egotiation between the committee and the [Judicial Conference's four-member] task force [that] proceeded for several months, often on a daily basis."[74] The report raised strong criticisms of the judiciary's lobbying tactics and expressed concern that the judges had harmed the relationship between the judiciary and Congress:

The [Senate Judiciary] committee complied with the request of the Judicial Conference to work with one body [i.e., the four-judge task force appointed by Chief Justice Rehnquist], only to have the Conference seemingly defer to another body [i.e., the Conference's Committee on Judicial Improvements]—which had no role whatsoever in the discussions and negotiations—at the point of decision. Such actions only serve to undermine the cooperative relationship between Congress and the judicial branch that our citizens rightly expect and deserve.[75]

The senators' frank acknowledgment of their negotiations and cooperation with the judges in shaping the legislation confirms the power possessed by the Judicial Conference and the federal judiciary to influence Congress on matters of court reform. Moreover, the senators' relatively strong expression of anger at the contradictory signals communicated by the judiciary concerning the proposed court reform provisions indicates that the judges' effectiveness and credibility may be jeopardized when their judicial lobbying appears to the legislators to be inconsistent.

CONSEQUENCES OF THE JUDICIAL IMPROVEMENTS ACT

In the Judicial Improvements Act that was ultimately passed by Congress, the unified federal judiciary achieved its goals of gaining newly created judgeships and avoiding "micromanagement" instructions from Congress on how to conduct pretrial hearings. Instead of imposing precise requirements upon the district judges for their participation in pretrial conferences and other case management matters that have traditionally been controlled by judges' autonomous discretionary decisions, the act required all districts to develop their own plans for improving case-processing efficiency. According to the statute, individual district courts would control the court reform process themselves: "There shall be implemented by each United States district court, in accordance with this title, a civil justice expense and delay reduction plan" (28 U.S.C. § 471 (1991)), and, "[i]n formulating the provisions of its civil justice expense and delay reduction plan, each United States district court, in consultation with an advisory group . . . , shall consider and may include . . . litigation management and cost and delay reduction techniques [listed in the statute]" (28 U.S.C. § 473(b) (1991)).

The use of local advisory committees and the development of civil justice plans *within each individual district* instead of creating uniform national requirements effectively preserved the autonomy of judges in individual districts to shape court reform as it would affect their own courthouses. The judges could appoint trusted friends and supportive lawyers to the advisory committees to ensure that the recommendations produced by the committees would satisfy the district judges' needs and interests. Because judges remained in control of the advisory committees' composition and oversaw the recommendations produced by the committees, there was little risk that reforms would be proposed or introduced that lacked the wholehearted support of a district's judges.

By successfully resisting the recommendation of the Brookings Institution Task Force and Senator Biden's initial legislative proposal, the district judges remained firmly in control of civil litigation processes for their respective districts. However, even if Senator Biden's initial proposals had been enacted into law and thereby had required district judges to meet in conferences with litigants for every civil case, the fragmentation of power and discretionary authority of federal judges still would have given judicial officers the means to resist compliance with congressional directives with which they disagreed.

In fact, federal judges have so much discretionary authority and independence as life-tenure, Article III judicial officers that they can ignore their own court reform initiatives when compliance with such initiatives is inconvenient for them. For example, the U.S. District Court for the Northern District of Ohio was designated as one of four "demonstration courts" under the Civil Justice Reform Act, a subtitle of the Judicial Improvements Act of 1990. Along with the Northern District of California, the Western District of Michigan, and the Northern District of West Virginia, the Northern District of Ohio was "required to experiment with various methods of reducing cost and delay in civil litigation" in order to produce valuable innovations for later adoption by other district courts.[76] Presumably these districts volunteered for this responsibility, since two demonstration districts contained two of the most famous innovators among district court judges throughout the country, Judge Enslen of the Western District of Michigan and Chief Judge Thomas Lambros of the Northern District of Ohio.

The case management plan developed in the Northern District of Ohio by the judges and their advisory committee included new court rules concerning civil litigation and the use of alternative dispute resolution. Court Rule 8:4.2 requires that there be a "Case Management Conference" in order to facilitate discovery and discuss the suitability of a case for alternative dispute resolution processes (e.g., arbitration, mediation). According to the court rule adopted in December 1991, "[t]he Judicial Officer shall conduct the Case Management Conference." Under Rule 8:1.2(b), "Judicial Officer" is defined as either a U.S. district judge or a U.S. magistrate judge, and Rule 8:1.2(c) reiterates that the case management conference is "conducted by the Judicial Officer."[77] Despite the clarity of the court's rule concerning case management conferences, judges violate the rule when it suits their interests.

In 1993, the judges from the Northern District of Ohio and members of their advisory committee sponsored a series of "open forums" to gather feedback from the legal community and from the general public about the court reforms developed by the district court in the aftermath of the Judicial Improvements Act of 1990 and its constituent section entitled the Civil Justice Reform Act, which mandated the creation of district plans and advisory committees. At one open forum, a *pro se* litigator complained to the judges that a case management conference for his case was conducted by a district judge's law clerk rather than by a "Judicial Officer" (i.e., district judge or magistrate judge), as required by court rules. As the judges present at the forum expressed concern about the law clerk's reportedly impolite tone and behavior directed at the *pro se* litigator, Chief Judge Lambros matter-of-factly remarked that "many of my Case Management Conferences are conducted by my staff members."[78] The casual admission by the chief architect of the court reform rules for the district court that he ignores those rules when it suits his interests provided a telling example of the power of federal judges' discretion and independence and the way in which that discretion and independence determine what takes place in the judicial process.

The successful judicial efforts to shape the congressional court reform initiative also advanced the magistrates' interests. Although the magistrates began their judicial lobbying strategies as a defensive effort to stave off proposed legislation that threatened their authority, they ultimately exceeded their most optimistic expectations for expanding their status and authority. The Judicial Improvements Act of 1990 enhanced the magistrates' status as authoritative judicial officers. The act's "Definitions" section clearly endorsed the status and legitimacy of magistrates within the federal judiciary. Unlike the Brookings Institution Task Force report, which distinguished magistrates from "the judiciary," the Judicial Improvements Act stated emphatically that magistrates are officially members of the federal judiciary: "As used in this chapter, the term 'judicial officer' means a United States district court judge *or a United States magistrate*" (emphasis supplied).[79]

More important, the magistrates obtained their long-sought title change through a provision that was added as a so-called noncontroversial amendment that was never the subject of legislative hearings or debate. As a result of the enactment of the Judicial Improvements Act in December 1990, the subordinate judicial officers were to be known as "United States magistrate judges."[80] Although many of these judicial officers wanted to disassociate themselves completely from the term "magistrate," the new compromise title permitted them to begin calling themselves "Judges," and they began to do so even in courts in which district judges had previously forbidden them from calling themselves anything other than "Magistrates." The new title had the potential to give the magistrate judges more respect and credibility in the eyes of litigants and lawyers who do not understand the full breadth of magistrate judges' authority as federal judicial officers. In addition, the new title could help to increase magistrate judges' authority by encouraging more litigants to consent to have their civil cases heard by the district courts' subordinate judicial officers. The previous title, "Magistrate," may have deterred litigants from trusting magistrate judges' authority and effectiveness as trial judges: "Many litigants may automatically prefer to have their cases decided by someone bearing the title 'judge.' As a result, the magistrates los[t] opportunities to gain visibility and build their reputations as judicial officers, and the potential flexibility and judicial economy of the magistrate system [were] diminished."[81]

Senator Biden's original proposal to exclude magistrates from pretrial case management conferences was scrapped in favor of a more flexible provision requiring district courts to study their own procedures in order to develop plans for implementing effective case management practices. In addition, the legislation ultimately enacted by Congress in December 1990 advanced magistrates' goal of gaining greater actual authority by amending the Magistrates Act to permit district judges and magistrates to "advise the parties of the availability of [a] magistrate" for civil consent trials.[82] The statute previously prevented judicial officers from mentioning the consent trial option to litigants because of a fear that litigants might feel pressured to consent. Indeed, the risk that consents would not be entirely voluntary was evident in a study conducted by the Federal Judicial Center.[83]

By previously requiring all communications concerning consent to flow between the clerk of court and the litigants, Congress had sought to prevent any coercion of litigants by district judges who did not wish to hear a particular case or by magistrates who were eager to gain consents that would enable them to preside over trials. According to the House report on the 1979 Magistrates Act, which created magistrates' authority over consent trials:

The consent procedure is to be handled by the clerk of court. The response of the party is not to be conveyed to the district judge, and the district judge is not to attempt any inducement, subtle or otherwise, to encourage magistrate trials. This language is an important safeguard against what has been characterized as the "velvet blackjack" problem. Some judges may be tempted to force disfavored cases into disposition before magistrates by intimations of lengthy delays manufactured in district court if the parties exercise their right to stay in that court.[84]

Any communications regarding consent to a magistrate's jurisdiction were supposed to be exclusively between the clerk of court and the litigants, and the previous wording of the statute stated explicitly that "neither the district judge nor the magistrate shall attempt to persuade or induce any party to consent to reference of any civil matter to a magistrate."[85] However, because clerks in some districts did not diligently fulfill their responsibility to inform litigants about magistrates' authority over consent trials, under the statute's previous wording many litigants never even learned that they had the option of having their trial date accelerated by consenting to have a magistrate preside over the case.[86]

The new statutory language made it more likely that litigants would consent to have magistrates preside over their civil trials because there would be more opportunities for court personnel, including judges and magistrate judges, to inform—and persuade—litigants regarding the available options. If the enhanced ability to provide information to litigants resulted in more magistrate-supervised trials, the magistrates who enjoyed more opportunities to conduct trials would feel that they had moved closer to fulfillment of their complete authority under the Magistrates Act.

Through the Judicial Improvements Act, the magistrate judges attained the primary goals that motivated their National Council's lobbying interests. The title "Magistrate Judge" was probably the best title that they could hope for in light of the historic and continuing opposition by many district judges to proposals that would permit the judicial subordinates to be called "Judges" or "Associate Judges." The increased opportunities to educate litigants about the availability of magistrate judges for civil cases was certain to lead to more of the consent trials, which represent the most significant and desired exercise of broad judicial authority by the subordinate judicial officers. In addition, because magistrate judges' salaries and benefits nearly equaled those of district judges, Congress effectively conferred upon the lower tier of judicial officers the benefits, status, and authority that the magistrate judges strove to attain through their judicial lobbying.

CONCLUSION

When their interests were threatened by legislative proposals, the federal judiciary, including Article III judges and magistrate judges, reacted effectively. The federal judges counteracted the recommendations of Senator Biden and the Brookings Institution Task Force by putting forward alternative proposals that were developed jointly by influential members of the judiciary and the congressional judiciary committees. The federal judges also shaped the court reform legislation through their daily negotiations with the staff members from Senator Biden's Senate Judiciary Committee. Moreover, the federal judges retained control over court reform by moving the process of formulating reforms into individual district courts, where judges could control both the development and the implementation (or lack thereof) of court reform initiatives within their own courthouses.

Because the magistrate judges lacked the influence with Congress possessed by the Article III judges and the Judicial Conference, these subordinate judicial officers identified potential allies and lobbying strategies that could effectively influence congressional actions on court reform. As indicated by the events surrounding the development of the Judicial Improvements Act, the magistrate judges were ready and willing to employ their lobbying resources, but their legislative success stemmed primarily from the convergence of their interests with those of Article III judges and the Judicial Conference, who opposed Senator Biden's original legislation because it would have interfered with district judges' autonomy. While the members of the Senate Judiciary Committee were preoccupied by their negotiations with the Judicial Conference aimed at developing a bill that would be acceptable to both the judges and the court reformers within Congress, the magistrate judges' allies succeeded in adding specific provisions to the bill that advanced these subordinate officials' goals for attaining greater status and authority.

The political maneuvering underlying the Judicial Improvements Act illustrates the potential influence of federal judicial officers over court reform and judicial administration. Senator Biden's actions in initiating and sponsoring the Brookings Institution Task Force's proposal served the purpose of placing court reform on the policy agenda of Congress. However, when Senator Biden's proposals threatened the Article III judges' autonomy and the magistrate judges' status and authority, the federal judiciary swung into action to shape the reform legislation in ways that fit with the judicial officers' self-interest. Congress has traditionally been deferential to the federal judges when passing court reform legislation. The exceptions to this rule may reflect independent agendas of nonjudicial policy makers, as illustrated by the unhappiness of many federal judges with Congress's unwillingness to eliminate or revise drastically the U.S. Sentencing Guidelines.[87] Sentencing guidelines provide an outlet, both symbolic and practical, for policy makers to pursue goals concerning criminal punishment and equitable sentences that involve issues that extend beyond the less visible elements of court administration that judges can more readily shape and influence.

Congressional deference is partly the product of legislators' lack of both knowledge and keen interest in many matters concerning court organization and procedure. Such deference also reflects concerns about separation of powers and probably results from the overrepresentation of lawyers among the legislators. In the Ninety-Ninth Congress, for example, 251 of the 535 senators and representatives were lawyers.[88] According to Mark Miller's study comparing lawyers and nonlawyers in Congress, lawyer-legislators have more positive feelings toward the federal courts and are much less likely to believe that judges' decisions are motivated by politics.[89] Lawyers' affinity for and connections with the judiciary facilitate the dominance of legal professionals over policy decisions concerning the judicial branch of government. As a result, the federal judiciary effectively helps to shape court reform legislation. Thus, instead of including the proposals emanating from the respected Brookings Institution and the influential chairman of the Senate Judiciary Committee, which would have forced district judges to take greater personal responsibility for each case and thereby would have reduced the status and authority of magistrate judges, the legislation eventually enacted maintained judges' autonomy and enhanced magistrate judges' status.

NOTES

1. Immigration and Naturalization Service v. Chadha, 462 U.S. 919, 951 (1983).

2. U.S. Const., art. I, § 8, cl. 1 (taxing power); ibid., art. I, § 8, cl. 18 (Necessary and Proper Clause); ibid., art. I, § 9, cl. 7 (appropriations power).

3. Ibid., art. III, § 1.

4. See Deborah J. Barrow and Thomas G. Walker, *A Court Divided: The Fifth Circuit Court of Appeals and the Politics of Judicial Reform* (New Haven, Conn.: Yale University Press, 1988).

5. Stephen L. Wasby, "A Rich Historical Account", *Judicature* 72 (1989): 307.

6. J. Woodford Howard, *Courts of Appeals in the Federal Judicial System* (Princeton, N.J.: Princeton University Press, 1981), 90.

7. Barrow and Walker, 260.

8. Christopher E. Smith, *United States Magistrates in the Federal Courts: Subordinate Judges* (New York: Praeger, 1990), 168.

9. Malcolm M. Feeley, *Court Reform on Trial* (New York: Basic Books, 1983), 164.

10. Henry Glick, *Courts, Politics, and Justice*, 2d ed. (New York: McGraw-Hill, 1988), 41.

11. Feeley, 198.

12. 18 U.S.C. § 1913.

13. American Bar Association, *Code of Judicial Conduct*, Canon 4(B)(1983).

14. 18 U.S.C. § 1913.

15. Frank Coffin, "The Federalist Number 86: On Relations Between the Judiciary and Congress," in Robert A. Katzman, ed., *Judges and Legislators: Toward Institutional Comity*, 26–27 (Washington, D.C.: Brookings Institution, 1988).

16. Barrow and Walker, 259.

17. Robert A. Katzman, "The Underlying Concerns," in Robert A. Katzman, ed., *Judges and Legislators: Toward Institutional Comity*, 14–15 (Washington, D.C.: Brookings Institution, 1988).

18. Thomas G. Walker and Deborah J. Barrow, "Funding the Federal Judiciary: The Congressional Connection," *Judicature* 69 (1985): 46.

19. Ibid., 50.

20. Ibid., 46.

21. Peter Fish, *The Politics of Federal Judicial Administration* (Princeton, N.J.: Princeton University Press, 1973), 301–305.

22. Robert Carp and Ronald Stidham, *The Federal Courts*, 2d ed. (Washington, D.C.: Congressional Quarterly Press, 1991), 64.

23. Glick, 44.

24. David M. O'Brien, *Storm Center: The Supreme Court in American Politics*, 2d ed. (New York: W. W. Norton, 1990), 128.

25. Harry P. Stumpf, *American Judicial Politics* (San Diego, Calif.: Harcourt Brace Jovanovich, 1988), 142.

26. Robert Steamer, *Chief Justice: Leadership and the Supreme Court* (Columbia: University of South Carolina Press, 1986), 186.

27. O'Brien, 30.

28. John Brigham, *The Cult of the Court* (Philadelphia: Temple University Press, 1987), 99.

29. O'Brien, 130.

30. Linda Greenhouse, "Judges Challenge Rehnquist Action on the Death Penalty," *New York Times*, 6 October 1989, A1.

31. Ibid.

32. Fish, 306.

33. Statement of Chief Justice William H. Rehnquist (15 March 1989) (Press release provided by the Administrative Office of the U.S. Courts on behalf of the Judicial Conference of the United States).

34. John W. Winkler III, "Judges as Lobbyists: Habeas Corpus Reform in the 1940s," *Judicature* 68 (1985): 265.

35. See Prepared Remarks of Vice President Dan Quayle (Speech to the Annual Meeting of the American Bar Association, Atlanta, 13 August 1991); President's Council on Competitiveness, *Agenda for Civil Justice Reform in America* (Washington, D.C.: U.S. Government Printing Office, 1991); "Executive Order Implements Civil Justice Reforms," *The Third Branch* 11 (November 1991): 8.

36. Brookings Institution Task Force, *Justice for All: Reducing Costs and Delay in Civil Litigation* (Washington, D.C.: Brookings Institution, 1989), 28.

37. Christopher E. Smith, "The Development of a Judicial Office: United States Magistrates and the Struggle for Status," *Journal of the Legal Profession* 14 (1989): 183.

38. S. 2027, 101st Cong., 2d Sess. (1990).

39. Ibid., § 471(b)(3).

40. Ibid., § 471(b)(3)(I).

41 Statement of Senator Joseph Biden, *Congressional Record* 136 (daily ed. 25 Jan. 1990): S414.

42. Smith, *United States Magistrates*, 93.

43. Carroll Seron, "The Professional Project of Parajudges: The Case of the U.S. Magistrates," *Law and Society Review* 22 (1988): 569.

44. Carroll Seron, *The Roles of Magistrates: Nine Case Studies* (Washington, D.C.: Federal Judicial Center, 1985), 35–46.

45. Smith, *United States Magistrates*, 115–144.

46. Peter G. McCabe, "The Federal Magistrates Act of 1979," *Harvard Journal on Legislation* 16 (1979): 369.

47. Seron, "The Professional Project," 558 n.2.

48. Smith, *United States Magistrates*, 120.

49. Ibid., 168.

50. Administrative Office of the U.S. Courts, "Bankruptcy Judges, Magistrates Gain New Benefits; New Bankruptcy Judgeships Created," *The Third Branch* 20 (November 1988): 3.

51. Administrative Office of the U.S. Courts, "Congress Passes Bill to Increase Salaries, Limit Outside Income," *The Third Branch* 21 (November 1989): 1–2.

52. Committee on the Judicial Branch of the Judicial Conference of the United States, *Simple Fairness: The Case for Equitable Compensation of the Nation's Judges* (Washington, D.C.: Administrative Office of the U.S. Courts, 1988), 81–82.

53. Steven Puro and Roger A. Goldman, "U.S. Magistrates: Changing Dimensions of First-Echelon Federal Judicial Officers," in Philip DuBois, ed., *The Politics of Judicial Reform*, 141 (Lexington, Mass.: Lexington Books, 1982).

54. See David R. Mayhew, *Congress: The Electoral Connection* (New Haven, Conn.: Yale University Press, 1974), 13–77.

55. Christopher E. Smith, "Merit Selection Committees and the Politics of Appointing United States Magistrates," *Justice System Journal* 12 (1987): 213–214.

56. Smith, *United States Magistrates*, 80–81.

57. Judicial Conference of the United States, *The Federal Magistrates System: Report to Congress by the Judicial Conference of the United States* (Washington, D.C.: Administrative Office of the U.S. Courts, 1981), 60.

58. Smith, *United States Magistrates*, 80–81.

59. Smith, "The Development of a Judicial Office," 180–181.

60. Ibid., 183.

61. Smith, *United States Magistrates*, 185.

62. Seron, *The Roles of Magistrates*, 63.

63. Smith, "The Development of a Judicial Office," 184.

64. The official who provided a copy of the letter to the author granted permission for it to be quoted, but asked that the individuals who sent and received the letter not be identified by name.

65. "U.S. Magistrates: Part of the Problem or a Key to the Solution?" *Inside Litigation* 4 (February 1990): 1, 17.

66. Kay Lehman Schlozman and John T. Tierney, *Organized Interests and American Democracy* (New York: Harper & Row, 1986), 339.

67. Smith, "The Development of a Judicial Office," 194–195.

68. Federal Courts Study Committee, *Report of the Federal Courts Study Committee* (Washington, D.C.: Administrative Office of the U.S. Courts, 1990), 79.

69. *Prepared Statement of the Hon. Aubrey Robinson, Jr., Chief Judge of the U.S. District Court, District of the District of Columbia, Presented in Testimony Before the Senate Judiciary Committee During Consideration of S. 2027, The Civil Justice Reform Act of 1990*, 101st Cong., 2d Sess. (1990), 220.

70. *Prepared Statement of the Hon. Richard Enslen, U.S. District Judge for the Western District of Michigan, Presented During Testimony Before the Senate Judiciary Committee During Consideration of S. 2027, The Civil Justice Reform Act of 1990*, 101st Cong., 2d Sess. (1990), 276.

71. Administrative Office of the U.S. Courts, "Judicial Conference Acts on Habeas Corpus/Civil Reform," *The Third Branch* 22 (April 1990): 1.

72. Barrow and Walker, 255; Fish, 324.

73. Pub. L. No. 101–650, 104 Stat. 5089 (1990).

74. Senate Report No. 416, 101st Cong., 2d Sess. (1990), 4.

75. Ibid., 5.

76. "Civil Justice Reform Act Status Report Sent to Congress," *The Third Branch* 24 (July 1993): 4.

77. *Differentiated Case Management Plan of the United States District Court for the Northern District of Ohio* (13 December 1991), 29, 35.

78. Remarks of Chief Judge Thomas Lambros (Open Forum on Civil Justice Reform, Canton, Ohio, 22 September 1993) (observed by author and recorded in author's notes).

79. 28 U.S.C. § 482 (1990).

80. Judicial Improvements Act of 1990, Pub. L. 101–650 § 321, 104 Stat. 5089, 5117 (1990).

81. Smith, "The Development of a Judicial Office," 182.

82. 28 U.S.C. § 636(c)(2) (1990).

83. Seron, *The Roles of Magistrates*, 61–62.

84. House Report No. 1364, 95th Cong., 2d Sess. (1978), 13–14.

85. 28 U.S.C. § 636(c)(2) (1982).

86. Smith, *United States Magistrates*, 85.

87. See Jack B. Weinstein, "Learning, Speaking, and Acting: What Are the Limits for Judges?" *Judicature* 77 (1994): 328.

88. Roger H. Davidson and Walter J. Oleszek, *Congress and Its Members*, 2d ed. (Washington, D.C.: Congressional Quarterly Press, 1985), 110.

89. Mark C. Miller, "Lawyers in Congress: What Difference Does It Make?" *Congress & the Presidency* 20 (1993): 1–23.

3

Judicial Salaries

March 15, 1989, was a notable day in the history of the federal courts. Its historic importance was not due to any important judicial decision; rather, it was because Chief Justice William Rehnquist held a news conference at the Supreme Court. According to the *New York Times*, "It was the first news conference any Supreme Court Justice has ever held at the Court to discuss any subject other than his own imminent retirement."[1] The news conference concerned, according to Chief Justice Rehnquist, "the most serious threat to the future of the Judiciary and its continued operations that I have observed."[2] The subject that engendered this attention and emphasis from the chief justice was the inadequacy of salaries paid to federal judges. Chief Justice Rehnquist's press conference served to highlight the contents of a report produced by a committee of federal judges that made a variety of arguments in favor of salary increases for the federal judiciary.[3]

The Compensation Clause of the Constitution protects judges from having their salaries reduced. Article III of the Constitution provides that "[t]he Judges, both of the supreme and inferior Courts, shall hold their Offices during good Behaviour, and shall, at stated Times, receive for their Services a Compensation, which shall not be diminished during their Continuance in Office." The Compensation Clause is obviously intended to insulate the judiciary from pressure by the other branches of government and thereby protect judicial independence. Although federal judges are protected against salary cuts, they must depend on the policy-making processes in the other branches of government for salary increases.

As the press conference by Chief Justice Rehnquist demonstrated, federal judges actively entered the policy-making process on behalf of their desired salary increases. Chief Justice Rehnquist's public lobbying for salary increases was unanimously supported by the Judicial Conference of the United States, a body of federal judges representing circuits and districts throughout the United States, which makes recommendations to Congress on behalf of the judiciary. The anomalous nature of a public relations blitz by federal judicial officers underscored the importance that federal judges attached to the compensation issue in the aftermath of congressional rejection of pay raises that were originally expected to be implemented in 1989. Federal judges lobbied for legislation to provide immediate 30 percent salary increases, along with periodic cost-of-living adjustments. This proposal was less lucrative than the 50 percent increases recommended by the 1988 Quadrennial Commission and subsequently rejected by Congress, but more generous than the other legislative proposals put forward in the House of Representatives.

Because it is relatively unusual for federal judges to shed their traditional judicial role of neutrality and restraint in order to manifest unabashed, visible self-interest in lobbying publicly for legislation, it is important to examine the arguments presented to justify these salary increase proposals, which were obviously of supreme importance to members of the judiciary. Although the judges' arguments were couched in terms of providing protection for the institution of the judiciary and restoring a modest degree of fairness in compensating hard-working public servants, whenever authoritative governmental officials advocate measures affecting their own personal financial interests, these measures deserve the utmost critical scrutiny. Because the salary issue presents one of the clearest examples of judges pursuing their own self-interest, this chapter will examine the arguments presented to justify federal judges' desired salary increases and attempt to analyze the broader implications and consequences of judicial compensation as a component of judges' perspectives and influence over judicial administration.

FEDERAL JUDICIAL SALARIES: BACKGROUND

In an attempt to make fair decisions about compensation for high-ranking governmental officials and reduce the political battles that inevitably surround salary decisions for such officials, Congress created the Commission on Executive, Legislative, and Judicial Salaries in 1967.[4] The commission, commonly referred to as the Quadrennial Commission, was composed of members appointed by the president, by leaders of the Senate and House of Representatives, and by the chief justice of the Supreme Court.[5] Every four years the Quadrennial Commission made salary recommendations for members of Congress, federal judges, and high-ranking executive branch officials. These recommendations were sent to the president, who subsequently made final recommendations to Congress. The president's recommendations, presumably based upon and legitimized by the "nonpolitical" calculations of the Quadrennial Commission, became effective unless they were rejected by Congress.[6]

An examination of the Quadrennial Commission's history shows that its recommendations were usually either reduced by the president or rejected by Congress. The work of the 1968 and 1976 Quadrennial Commissions led to salary increases, albeit not quite at the recommended levels. The recommendations in 1972 and 1980 resulted in no increases in compensation for the affected officials and judges.[7] From the judges' perspective, a central problem with the procedures was that the judges' salary increases were tied to pay raises for members of Congress. Thus judicial salaries suffered the consequences of adverse public reactions to pay increases for legislators. The efforts advocated by Chief Justice Rehnquist and other judicial officials in 1989 for raising judges' salaries represented an attempt to separate consideration of their compensation from that of members of Congress and thereby diminish the harmful consequences for the judges of public scrutiny and opposition to congressional pay raises.

This effort to remove the links between congressional and judicial pay raises was based on more than pragmatic recognition of the detrimental political consequences of considering salaries as part of a single package. Judges serve a very different function than members of Congress. Judges require specific advanced education and legal expertise. Judges also have significant restrictions upon their ability to earn outside income.[8] In addition, unlike members of Congress, judges cannot determine their own salaries. Thus there was ample reason to consider judicial salaries, as well as those of executive branch officials, separately from the congressional salaries evaluated in the same Quadrennial Commission process.

JUDGES AND INFLATION

A variety of arguments were put forward to justify salary increases for federal judges. The arguments flowed from the deep dissatisfaction felt by federal judges about their levels of compensation. The most compelling justification for an increase in judicial salaries was the universally acknowledged fact that because judges' pay had not kept pace with inflation, they had suffered a loss of income in real economic terms. Judge Richard Posner's systematic examination of federal judicial salaries since 1800 demonstrated that, when dollar values are held constant, judges' salaries peaked in 1969 and declined in value thereafter, due to inflationary pressures.[9] During the 1970s, more than 140 federal judges who were angry at the erosion in their compensation caused by inflation (and congressional inaction) joined together to file a lawsuit claiming that their salaries had been unconstitutionally reduced by Congress's failure to address the impact of inflation upon their salaries.[10] Their legal action was rejected by the U.S. Court of Claims,[11] but the fact that they initiated a legal action reflected the depth of their feeling about the issue.

In 1989, the federal judges, not surprisingly, built their arguments by using the peak value of their 1969 salaries as a reference point. By using the peak salary value as a reference point, Chief Justice Rehnquist could assert before a congressional committee that the proposed salary increase "is not, in my view, fairly termed a pay 'raise.' "[12] By 1988, federal district and circuit judges' salaries had lost 30 percent of their value since 1969.[13] Supreme Court justices suffered a 43 percent loss in real income over the same time period.[14] The salary gains of military personnel, other federal employees, and workers in private industry outpaced the judges' compensation gains after 1969.[15] Because this reduction in salary value is not an unconstitutional diminution of salary under the Compensation Clause of the Constitution that would be remediable by court order,[16] inflation has been a continual problem as judges have depended on Congress to recognize and remedy the pressures attendant to changing economic conditions. The framers of the Constitution foresaw the difficulties that inflation would pose for judicial salaries, but they rejected James Madison's plan for indexing judges' pay to inflation.[17]

The inflation-induced reduction in the value of judicial salaries, particularly when the real disposable income of most other Americans generally had increased over the past century,[18] violated the judges' reasonable expectation that their salaries would not be reduced *de facto* through economic forces that were not similarly affecting other Americans. Thus federal judges could make a particularly strong argument for the cost-of-living adjustments that they sought in their legislative proposal.

This persuasive justification for offsetting inflation did not, however, provide a basis for setting the judges' salary level or granting a particular raise. The salary levels of federal judges in 1989 were $89,500 for district court judges, $95,000 for circuit court of appeals judges, $110,000 for Supreme Court associate justices, and $115,000 for the chief justice.[19] Because these salaries were more than three times greater than the median income for *households* nationwide ($28,906), including households with more than one wage earner,[20] the question remains whether federal judges should really have been considered underpaid.

THE RISK OF RESIGNATIONS

Chief Justice Rehnquist claimed that unhappiness with salaries could lead many federal judges to resign. There was no doubt that a massive exodus of experienced judges would have had a detrimental impact upon the federal courts' ability to process cases. This was especially true because of the lengthy socialization period required for new judges, particularly district judges, to learn their jobs.[21] In addition, when judges leave the bench, it can frequently take months to replace them through the slow appointment process, as the executive branch, bar association, and legislative branch each investigates and examines the nominees. In a 1988 survey of federal judges, a significant number of judges indicated that their dissatisfaction with salaries had led them to consider resigning, taking early retirement, or electing senior status at an earlier date than originally planned.[22]

Based upon the survey results, it appeared that there was a great risk that judges would begin to leave the judiciary because their salary expectations were not being met. The survey, which was conducted on behalf of the judiciary, was clearly designed to illuminate the judges' opinions about compensation problems and thereby provide an opportunity for judicial officers to express their dissatisfaction. These opinions did not, however, necessarily translate into actions. The judges' own report advocating salary increases provided evidence that compensation concerns had not had a significant impact upon departures from the judiciary. There were indications that dissatisfaction with salaries contributed to twenty-three of the twenty-six resignations during the preceding ten years.[23] However, an increase in resignations and retirements from fewer than one judge per year in the early 1970s to an average of five to six judges each year in the late 1980s could hardly be called significant or detrimental to the judicial branch. This was an especially small number of judges, especially when viewed in light of the judiciary's size increase from 423 judges to 712 judges during that same time span.[24]

It is instructive to note that even in 1970, when district judges' salaries of $60,000 were just below their 1969 peak value and were more than six times greater than the median family income of $9,867,[25] there were still two resignations.[26] These resignations at the height of judges' financial prosperity constituted percentage losses equivalent to the losses to the federal judiciary from resignations in every one of the years from 1979 through 1983 when the judges' salaries had much lower economic values. For example, the resignations in 1970 constituted a loss of nearly 0.5 percent, while the three resignations in 1983 constituted an identical loss because of the increase in district and appellate judgeships. While a risk of accelerated departures existed, the evidence does not show that the harm materialized—despite the fact that dissatisfaction with salaries had been a persistent complaint of judges for many decades, dating back to the 1920s.[27]

Moreover, a comprehensive study conducted in the 1990s on the resignations by all federal judges from the beginning of the federal courts in 1789 through 1992 showed that only 21 of 127 resignations over the 200-year period were actually attributable to dissatisfaction with salaries. According to Emily Van Tassel, a historian for the federal courts' own Federal Judicial Center,

[T]he Commission on Executive, Legislative and Judicial Salaries (known as the Quadrennial Commission) reiterated in several reports the assertion that judicial resignations because of inadequate salary during the 1970s and 1980s exceeded all judicial resignations for all reasons combined for the preceding 200 years. Although a close look at the history of judicial resignations proves the statement to be inaccurate, the sentiment suggests the depth of concern that the salary issue evoked.[28]

During his press conference, Chief Justice Rehnquist expressed the concern that the federal judiciary should not become like state judiciaries, in which judges serve for five or ten years and then move into lucrative private practice. When asked by reporters why this was so important, the chief justice responded with a heartfelt, but vague, answer that federal judgeships are supposed to be "lifetime careers" rather than a stepping stone to other positions. The chief justice never clearly articulated why this was important; he merely conveyed the message that the thought of federal judges leaving the bench clashed with his expectations and was "not the concept that has prevailed with the federal judiciary."[29] He cited no particular harm to the judiciary, and indeed, based upon the low number of departures, it would have been very difficult for him to argue about anything other than a mere risk of harm. Moreover, Judge Posner, an ally of Rehnquist's as an advocate of salary increases, contradicted this argument by concluding that dissatisfaction with salaries would not lead to departures from the federal judiciary. The average age at appointment for federal judges is fifty, and these appointees are aware of likely future salary conditions. According to Judge Posner, these facts diminish the likelihood of judicial resignations because "few people have a taste for switching careers after age 60, especially since the financial attractiveness of a federal judgeship increases as retirement age approaches."[30]

THE RECRUITMENT OF ELITE LAWYERS AS JUDGES

In Judge Posner's view, "[t]he problem with inadequate salaries is not that they can be expected to trigger an avalanche of resignations, but rather . . . that they limit the field of selection."[31] The Committee on the Judicial Branch echoed Judge Posner's concern by stating that "[t]here is every reason to believe that the position of Federal judge has become less attractive to prospective appointees because of low judicial salaries."[32] The committee, like other commentators,[33] provided only anecdotal evidence about the deterrent effect of judicial salaries upon potential appointees.

There are several reasons to be skeptical about the detrimental consequences of this putative phenomenon. First, there are large numbers of judges who take significant pay cuts in order to assume judicial office. According to the judges' own statistics, "73 percent of judges now on the bench took a pay cut when appointed, and . . . the average salary reduction was $69,708."[34] This indicates that for many appointees the status, authority, autonomy, and power inherent in service on the federal bench outweigh simple calculations of personal income potential. In addition, the generous retirement benefits for federal judges may be an attractive incentive for some lawyers, even if a judgeship would require a loss of income. Federal judges can retire with full pay at age seventy with ten years' service or at age sixty-five with fifteen years' service. By becoming "senior judges," they can work as much or little as they wish and still receive the benefits of any subsequent pay raises.[35]

Because it is clear that judgeships are sufficiently attractive to induce lawyers to reduce their incomes in order to join the federal bench, the primary question concerned precisely which lawyers may have been deterred from accepting appointments. Clearly Judge Posner was concerned that the federal judiciary would lose access to high-income private practitioners as potential appointees.[36] In order to attract these candidates, economic analysts have argued that judicial salaries should be set at some unspecified optimal level in order to maximize the attraction of qualified lawyers to the federal bench.[37] As a practical matter, however, can the government attempt to compete with salaries in excess of several hundred thousand dollars in order to attract candidates from the elite private bar? In an era of budget deficits and spending cuts in governmental programs, there would be little reason to use substantial salary increases in an attempt to attract such high-income lawyers to the federal bench unless there was a demonstrable harm from having lower salaries.

One reason why it was difficult to demonstrate the harm of salaries substantially lower than those enjoyed at the top of the legal profession is that there is never a shortage of interested, qualified candidates for judgeships. Unlike some governmental positions that require specific technical skills possessed by only a few people, such as research scientists and nuclear reactor inspectors, for whose services the government has a tremendous incentive to compete with private industry, there are many lawyers who could be appointed to the federal bench. This is not to say that any lawyer would make a good federal judge, but with the national pool of lawyers estimated to exceed 700,000 in number, there will always be thousands of capable, qualified, and experienced candidates available to fill the 800 federal judgeships—only a portion of which are vacant at any given time. In addition to the apparently large pool of private practitioners who would accept a federal judgeship whether or not it required a loss of income, there are many public sector legal professionals, including prosecutors, state judges, and U.S. magistrate judges, who would see their incomes rise by joining the federal bench.

Despite his recognition that many lawyers in each district would be regarded as qualified by the American Bar Association's Standing Committee on the Judiciary, Judge Posner took issue with the notion that there are many candidates available to fill federal judgeships:

There may be a dozen people who are well qualified by intellect, character, and temperament to fill a particular vacancy on the federal bench, yet of those all but two or three may be disqualified because they have the wrong ideology or political connections or live in the wrong state or district. Any further narrowing of the field because of inadequate salary could have a substantial adverse impact on the quality of appointments.[38]

Judge Posner was quite right to acknowledge the role of politics in determining federal judicial appointments, but he overestimated the emphasis on the quality of candidates. Moreover, his reliance on the ABA Standing Committee's judgments regarding qualifications highlighted the problems involved in determining which lawyers are qualified, especially when viewed in light of the ABA Standing Committee's split vote over Judge Bork's judicial qualifications to be a Supreme Court justice in 1987. In evaluating Judge Bork, ten members of the ABA Standing Committee rated him well qualified, four members rated him not qualified, and one member voted "not opposed."[39] Obviously, there is no clear consensus about what qualities make someone qualified to be a federal judge.

As numerous examples show, presidents and senators can manifest a shocking disregard for considerations of quality, a criterion that Judge Posner assumes to exist in selecting judicial nominees, when appointing federal judges. For example, President Ronald Reagan's nominations of Jefferson Sessions and Daniel Manion quite rightly attracted questions regarding the experience (or lack thereof) and attitudes that these judicial nominees would be bringing to the federal bench. Sessions, a former Alabama U.S. attorney, had called the NAACP and the American Civil Liberties Union "un-American" and "communist-inspired." Manion, an appointee to the Seventh Circuit Court of Appeals, was approved by a margin of only one vote in the Senate because he completely lacked judicial experience, federal court litigation experience, and any record of legal scholarship. In addition, the briefs he submitted to support his confirmation were characterized as weak in spelling and grammar.[40]

Because appointments have been based upon a wide variety of considerations, including ideology and patronage, the actual pool of potential candidates is probably much broader than Judge Posner believed it to be. This is not an argument favoring an absence of qualitative evaluations for judicial appointees, but rather an observation that the realities of the political selection system emphasize a different mixture of criteria for each nominee. Judge Posner claimed that there were only a few qualified and eligible candidates for each vacancy.[41] In reality, however, districts in virtually every state contain private practitioners, state judges, government attorneys, lawyer-politicians, and law professors who possess a desirable combination of legal qualifications and partisan political credentials that makes them plausible appointees under the current selection system.

As Judge Posner acknowledged[42] and history has shown, certain lawyers in private practice with stratospheric salaries may never be attracted to any salary that the government could reasonably afford to offer. For example, John W. Davis, the former presidential candidate and solicitor general, whose Wall Street law practice earned him $275,000 even in the worst years of the Depression,[43] declined an appointment to the Supreme Court because, as he said, "I have taken the vows of chastity and obedience but not of poverty."[44] Thus the field of potential appointees is inevitably narrowed because of the disparity between lawyers' and judges' salaries. As the foregoing discussion indicates, however, this narrowing of the universe of potential candidates will not cause the detrimental consequences envisioned by Judge Posner because his presumption that there are only two or three qualified, eligible candidates for each judicial vacancy underestimated the pool of qualified attorneys and misjudged the actual criteria that guide judicial appointments.

JUDGES' REFERENCE GROUPS

In making arguments about why they should receive significant raises, federal judges compared themselves to other judges, lawyers, and law professors.[45] However, virtually the only public-sector employees whose salaries could match the incomes of $300,000 or more enjoyed by partners in large-city law firms are college football and basketball coaches—state university employees responsible for generating massive amounts of revenue for their institutions. It is indeed incongruous that sports coaches are valued more highly than judges in regard to compensation, but these public employees are, in effect, expected to pay their own salaries by generating revenues. Moreover, their excessive salaries seem partially intended to offset their lack of job security. Judges, although more valuable to society, are not similarly situated to receive such high salaries. Judges have very different responsibilities, which do not include generating revenues for the government.

Federal judges noted that their salaries were lower than those of their counterparts in Great Britain and Canada. For example, trial judges in Great Britain earned $117,000, and comparable judges in Canada were paid $106,000, figures that exceeded federal district judges' $89,500.[46] However, these comparisons failed to discuss the higher cost-of-living rates and higher income tax rates in those countries, which significantly reduced the relative value of the foreign judges' salaries. During the 1980s, if the cost of living in Washington, D.C., were considered as the baseline of 100, London,

England's costs would be rated at 134 and Ottawa, Canada's costs would be rated at 119.[47] With respect to taxes, the top Canadian federal tax rate was 46 percent. The top individual tax rate in Great Britain was 60 percent. By contrast, the top federal tax rate in the United States was only 28 percent.[48]

Federal judicial salaries were matched or slightly exceeded by judges' salaries in three states. New York paid its highest appellate judges $115,000 and its trial court judges $95,000. California paid its appellate judges $97,000, and Michigan paid its appellate judges $96,000.[49] Such differences in salaries are an inherent risk in a system of federalism, in which states have the ability to control the salaries of their own employees.[50] Although it may be desirable for federal judges' salaries to remain ahead of or comparable to those of state judges because of the federal judiciary's greater prestige and authority, the determination of specific salaries is subject to the influence of the varied political forces within each respective governmental arena. Because of the divergent political climates and interests affecting various state governments, it may simply be easier to adjust some state judicial salaries without the political fragmentation and national media attention attendant to salary legislation in Congress.

Federal judges also compared themselves to another prestigious group of lawyers with impressive credentials who voluntarily forego income in order to accept a public service–oriented position: law professors. Judges argued that the salaries of deans and professors at the nation's top twenty-five law schools exceeded those of federal judges.[51] As with state judges, it may be desirable to maintain judicial salaries ahead of or comparable to academic salaries. Unlike judicial salaries, academic salaries are affected by market forces.

Theoretically, professors can compare offers from different law schools and negotiate their compensation packages. In reality, however, there is little job mobility for professors who do not teach at elite law schools. Most professors have few opportunities to take advantage of market forces as a means to increase their salaries. Thus judicial salaries exceeded the salaries of the majority of professors and the differences between the salaries of the highest-paid professors and those of the federal judges were not great. In 1989, the average salary for a law professor at the full-professor level was $74,544. and, at the assistant-professor level, it was only $42,688.[52] These figures were below the $89,500 figure for federal district judges. In addition, the accoutrements of judicial office, including prestige, authority, and generous retirement benefits, made federal judgeships more attractive than law professorships. There was no evidence that professors turned down judgeships or that judges left the bench in large numbers in order to become professors.

ASSESSING JUDICIAL SALARIES FROM
A SOCIETAL PERSPECTIVE

The arguments favoring increased compensation for federal judges tended to have a "microscopic" quality in focusing very narrowly upon the federal judges' self-interest and frustrations. By placing the justifications for salary increases under the lens of broader society, the more important implications and consequences of the debate over judicial compensation can be illuminated.

It is easy to understand the federal judges' frustrations at seeing their purchasing power decline significantly over a period of two decades. The judges who relied upon the 1969 peak salary value could reasonably have hoped that Congress would maintain their real compensation levels according to the "moral duty" that, according to one commentator's characterization,[53] the legislative branch has to maintain the vitality of the Compensation Clause's prohibition against diminution of judicial salaries. It is less clear that judges appointed since 1969 should have possessed precisely the same expectation. When Chief Justice Rehnquist characterized the proposed 30 percent salary increase as a "partial recapture of . . . purchasing power" and "not . . . a pay 'raise,' "[54] he spoke as if all federal judges had suffered from a tremendous decline in the value of their judicial salaries. In fact, the vast majority of the judges serving at that time were appointed during the immediately preceding years of the Carter and Reagan administrations when judicial salaries had already clearly fallen below their peak level. Thus, although their frustration at steadily suffering the effects of inflation was understandable, they should not have possessed the same reasonable expectations for recapturing lost salary value as their senior colleagues.

While some level of dissatisfaction and anxiety about the effects of the political process upon future pay raises was understandable, the manner in which some judges characterized their situation was quite revealing. In portraying their financial situation as desperate, essentially because they primarily compared themselves with the elite private bar as the most relevant reference group, the judges indicated how removed they were from the travails of life that affected their fellow citizens.

It was clear, particularly from the concerns raised by Judge Posner, that the primary reference group for federal judges was the elite private bar. As the judges' own report to the Quadrennial Commission stated, "Because judicial nominees who join the bench from private law firms are generally drawn from the top ranks of practice, we believe salaries for the top ten percent of law firm partners provide the most relevant measure of comparison to Federal judicial salaries."[55] Thus, the degree of dissatisfaction was not a function of actual economic suffering, at least not the kind of struggles to obtain the necessities of housing, medical care, transportation, and education that affect millions of Americans who are middle-class or below, but rather was the result of a substantial gap between financial expectations and the actual economic rewards of judicial service. Because federal judges could see the affluence enjoyed by their law school classmates who remained in private practice, they were keenly aware of the benefits they could enjoy at any moment that they decided to take off their black robes.

The judges' self-comparison to the elite law firms' salaries was continually reinforced to the judges when they saw their law clerks, inexperienced attorneys who worked under their supervision, receive pay higher than judges' salaries soon after leaving the federal court to work in private practice.[56] The elite-lawyer reference group kept many judges' eyes focused upon the peak of society; they did not see and understand the lives of the vast majority of Americans who live on the broad plane at the base of American society's economic pyramid.

Several comments made by judges to justify salary increases instructively illuminated this problem. One anonymous respondent to the federal judges' survey, whose response was prominently quoted in the judges' committee report advocating pay raises, said, " 'The long term financial sacrifice for my family is too much. I cannot sentence them to a lifetime of genteel *poverty*' " (emphasis supplied).[57] In reality, it was quite revealing for anyone earning at least $89,500 annually, a sum that was over four times greater than the median salary for full-time American workers,[58] to speak about living in "poverty." Not only was this characterization inconsistent with the fact that millions of Americans at that time were unemployed, homeless, and/or lacking medical insurance, but also it demonstrated an absence of sensitivity to the harsh realities of life in American society and the undeniably privileged position enjoyed by citizens who receive the relatively high salaries of federal judges.

When asked at the press conference whether the federal government should try to match private law firm salaries, Chief Justice Rehnquist recognized the indisputable fact that it would be entirely unreasonable to expect judicial salaries to approach the extremely high salaries enjoyed by lawyers in private practice. The chief justice added, however, that the government should "offer [judges] enough so that they will be able to educate their kids."[59] The chief justice was highlighting a problem that received strong emphasis in the judges' arguments favoring salary increases—namely, the escalating costs of college which affect the federal judiciary because of the age at which judges join the bench.

According to the judges' report, "[t]he average age of Federal judges at appointment has for years hovered around age 50. This is an age at which many parents have children of college age and thus encounter the largest tuition-related financial strains." [60] According to the judges' committee, "[f]or Federal judges today, assisting their children through college imposes a tremendous hardship. Sending them to graduate school—helping them to pursue the same career paths the judges themselves have chosen—may simply be out of reach."[61] Although it is true that college costs have escalated dramatically over the past two decades,[62] Chief Justice Rehnquist's statement and those in the judges' committee report evinced no understanding of or even curiosity about what the rest of their fellow citizens had to do in order to educate their children. Compared to the majority of Americans, judges have extremely high incomes. According to figures from the Census Bureau, only the top 5.3 percent of American families shared the federal judges' annual income level of $90,000 or more in 1989.[63]

Moreover, many federal judges have significant financial assets and investment income that they bring to the judiciary with them, on top of their annual salaries, as a result of coming from affluent families or of working in lucrative legal and business careers prior to service on the bench. Compared to the rest of American society, judges' investment holdings constitute significant financial resources that supplement their relatively high salaries. As indicated by the following lists of federal district and circuit judges in Ohio and U.S. Supreme Court justices, federal judges are required to report their holdings as within a range rather than as a specific amount. These amounts do not indicate the judicial officers' net worths, which would be even higher because judges are allowed to exclude the value of their personal residences and their personal property.

U.S. Supreme Court Justices, 1992[64]

Sandra Day O'Connor	$1.77 million to $4.53 million
John Paul Stevens	$1.13 million to $2.5 million
Harry Blackmun	$300,000 to $830,000
Antonin Scalia	$265,000 to $565,000
William Rehnquist	$255,000 to $725,000
Anthony Kennedy	$245,000 to $920,000
Byron White	$165,000 to $415,000
Clarence Thomas	$65,000 to $165,000
David Souter	$65,000 to $150,000

Ohio Circuit Judges, 1989[65]

Leroy J. Contie, Jr.	$742,000 to $1.77 million
David A. Nelson	$638,047 to $1.38 million
Paul C. Weick	$537,683 to $694,168
Alan E. Norris	$254,010 to $686,000
George C. Edwards, Jr.	$136,011 to $375,000
Nathaniel R. Jones	$32,004 to $110,000
Anthony J. Celebrezze	$20,002 to $65,000

Ohio District Judges, 1989[66]

Alvin I. Krenzler	$2.43 million to $3.83 million
James L. Graham	$1.4 million to $1.64 million
S. Arthur Spiegel	$370,118 to $1.01 million
Ann Aldrich	$334,004 to $455,001
John Holschuh	$282,000 to $710,000
Alice Batchelder	$252,007 to $605,000
Joseph P. Kinneary	$180,005 to $400,000
John W. Potter	$136,022 to $446,000
William K. Thomas	$120,519 to $385,000
Thomas D. Lambros	$118,006 to $265,000
Sam Bell	$97,009 to $325,000
Herman J. Weber	$70,006 to $232,000
Richard B. McQuade, Jr.	$57,007 to $190,000
Don Young	$41,005 to $135,000
David S. Porter	$40,004 to $130,000
Frank J. Battisti	$33,007 to $110,000
Carl B. Rubin	$31,009 to $110,000
Walter H. Rice	$21,207 to $64,500
Nicholas J. Walinski	$21,003 to $70,000
John M. Manos	$20,002 to $65,000
David Dowd	$16,002 to $55,000
George H. White	$15,001 to $50,000

When viewed in light of the judges' arguments about living in "genteel poverty" or being unable to afford to send their children to college, the comparison of judges' salaries with those of most Americans and the recognition that judges frequently possess additional financial resources raise a question: If judges are struggling with the cost of education, what must their fellow citizens be facing? It was apparent that in seeking to gain raises for themselves, the judges were not pondering, and indeed not even recognizing, how life must be for the nearly 95 percent of American households with lower annual incomes—households containing the citizens whose lives are affected by the judges' decisions.

The clear message from the judges' statements was that federal judges were having to struggle a bit to achieve the level of material comfort that they expected. Their dissatisfaction was exacerbated because their expectations were based upon or at least influenced by the pinnacle of affluence that they observed, and knew could be available to them, in the elite private bar. Thus judges found themselves in the undesired and unexpected position of having to save and borrow money for their children's education, scale down expectations for houses and vacation homes, and juggle finances like the majority of Americans—except that judges had a significantly easier time of it because their salaries were so high compared to the rest of society.

Because judges' salaries were already firmly established at a level several times above the median salaries for other Americans, was there anything wrong with judges having to endure some element of economic struggle in attempting to attain their financial goals? In other words, should society seek to have judicial salaries chase after soaring private-sector salaries and thereby insulate judges from financial pressures?

Although one might argue that we should seek to insulate judges from financial pressures so that they are not distracted from their important judicial duties, the previously quoted statements of Chief Justice Rehnquist and the anonymous survey respondent about being unable to pay for children's education and living in "genteel poverty" indicate that there are grave risks in insulating judges through complete financial security. The judges lose touch with the social conditions and forces that affect the lives of their fellow citizens.

For example, from the desperate tone of the judges' complaints about salaries in 1989, one would never have guessed that the judges received cost-of-living increases in 1987 amounting to nearly $10,000 for district and circuit judges,[67] but their fellow citizens who supported themselves in minimum wage jobs had not received any raise from $3.35 per hour since 1981.[68] As one member of Congress observed during the 1989 controversy about raises for members of Congress and federal judges, "Could I feed my family on $3.35 an hour? . . . I can't even feed my family on $89,500, much less $3.35 an hour."[69] Not surprisingly, none of the federal judges publicly noted this comparison to minimum-wage workers in lobbying for their own salary increases. Such a comparison would not have advanced the self-interested focus of the judges' arguments. As a result, the judges' arguments made them appear to be out of touch with the society affected by their decisions.

The importance of keeping judges in contact with society has been made clear in twentieth-century jurisprudential developments concerning the nature of law in society. Only naive observers could believe that the development and application of law by judges is based upon a fixed, coherent system of legal principles. Influential legal scholars and jurists, going back to Pound, Holmes, Cardozo, and Brandeis, have recognized that judges develop law and concomitant policies by utilizing their values, observations, and understandings about society in addition to the traditional legal tools of *stare decisis* and formal legal theory. A significant body of scholarly research has documented how factors such as judges' backgrounds, values, and experiences influence the outcomes of judicial decision making.[70]

Much has been written about the manner in which the legal profession and the judicial system, as with other institutions in society, favor, if not serve, the affluent and politically powerful.[71] The insensitivity of federal judges to the struggles of their fellow citizens, a lack of understanding that was reinforced by their elite reference group and myopic justifications for salary increases is evident in many cases. For example, despite the fact that the courts are a branch of government that theoretically should provide a forum for the claims of all citizens, federal judges have decided several cases upholding strict financial barriers to court access, which can significantly affect the ability of less affluent people to gain access to and benefit from authoritative adjudicatory processes. Federal judges, for example, decided that people who cannot afford court filing fees cannot file for bankruptcy[72] or gain judicial review of a termination of welfare benefits.[73]

Federal judges are already drawn from the ranks of educated political elites. Reinforcement of their reference-group orientation toward the top economic stratum in society apparently only serves to exacerbate the legal system's relative lack of sensitivity and responsiveness to the lower strata of society. Judges who experience some of the trials and tribulations of daily life in American society and are not completely insulated from the pressures that face the average citizen should have a better ability to comprehend and address the human problems that confront the judiciary.

Chief Justice Rehnquist himself had said that judges must possess " 'common sense,' some patchwork of knowledge of the human condition gained from experience, or put some other way, the best judges undoubtedly have some sort of understanding of human nature and how the world works.' "[74] Yet the judges' self-interest in seeking salary increases appeared to blind them to the connections between their elite status in American society and their responsibility for understanding the lives of their fellow citizens. The judges sought insulation from the financial pressures that affect nearly all Americans, even though they were already near the top five percent of wage earners.

SECONDARY CONSEQUENCES OF THE JUDGES' SELF-INTEREST

The justices of the Supreme Court and, to a lesser degree, the other members of the federal judiciary represent a symbolic pinnacle of the legal profession. Although they do not possess the highest salaries, these judicial officers are the leaders of the legal profession in the eyes of law students and lawyers. The importance of federal judges as role models and leaders is evident in a number of respects: Legal education is devoted to studying the ideas and theories of federal judges; clerkships with federal judges are the most sought after positions for new lawyers; federal judges are the primary focus of scholarly research on the judicial system; and federal judges receive a substantial share of the news media's attention in any broadly disseminated discussions about law and the legal system. What message were members of the legal profession and aspiring lawyers receiving from the strong expressions of dissatisfaction with judicial salaries that were emanating from these legal role models in the federal judiciary?

A primary, unmistakable message from Chief Justice Rehnquist's press conference and the salary concerns expressed by other federal judges was that experienced lawyers should legitimately expect to become wealthy. The federal judges endorsed and legitimized the highly paid, elite private bar as the focal point for the aspirations by lawyers and law students. By using the elite bar as their reference group for salaries, the judges were, by example, defining the material expectations that other lawyers should adopt as goals. The legitimation of the top stratum of the bar as the reference point for the aspirations of members of the legal profession has some potentially damaging effects.[75]

Most important, if federal judges can be legitimately dissatisfied with salaries that are several times greater than those of the majority of Americans, how should lawyers feel about accepting low-paying positions as public defenders or legal aid attorneys? If lawyers and law students are taught by the leaders of the legal profession that they should legitimately expect to become wealthy, who will fill the essential, but modestly compensated, legal positions providing representation to the poor? In fact, Chief Justice Rehnquist's press conference coincided with and probably reinforced the trend of law students moving away from public interest work in favor of jobs that would produce high incomes.[76] There will always be a few committed idealists to assume those roles of legal aid attorneys, but for other public-sector attorneys, who are taught to fix their aspirations upon the top of the legal profession, there will very quickly be a gap between their material expectations and their financial rewards. Thus the clients of low-paid legal aid attorneys will continue to be inadequately served as these positions remain a revolving door for an unending flow of inexperienced attorneys.

Perhaps this criticism of the judiciary seems a bit harsh because the values and images prevalent throughout American society, which influence federal judges as well as the rest of the citizenry, reinforce material aspirations and measure success in terms of affluence. In many respects, the federal judges were inevitably mere component parts in a larger economic and social system that encourages high financial expectations. They simply behaved as other Americans in seeking to gain whatever rewards they could from their service to society. Federal judges cannot be held responsible for the detrimental consequences of the values upon which American society was built.

In their roles as visible, symbolic leaders of the legal system, however, the federal judges chose to invest their energy and political power in pursuit of self-interested financial goals based upon myopic justifications. Chief Justice Rehnquist chose to hold his unique, historic press conference to seek salary increases for judges who were already highly paid in relation to the rest of American society. He used his position and stature to publicize speculative harms to the judiciary (e.g., the risk of increased resignations), rather than speaking about documentable problems concerning the lack of legal services for the poor or some other issue related to the judicial system that urgently required public attention. Judicial salaries deserved attention, particularly because of the continuing impact of inflation upon judges' purchasing power. But in using a historic press conference to legitimize lawyers' high financial expectations and to encourage the use of the elite bar as an appropriate reference group, the federal judges subtly reinforced lawyers' roles as profit-oriented business people, rather than their usual self-proclaimed public image as professionals providing service to society.

CONCLUSION

The federal judges succeeded in persuading Congress to grant them salary increases. The judges' lobbying produced a significant 25 percent pay increase plus additional cost-of-living increases of 7.9 percent, 3.6 percent, and 3.5 percent in succeeding years.[77] District judges' salaries increased from $89,500 in 1989 to $129,500 in 1992. Other federal judges received comparable raises: U.S. magistrate judges, $119,140; circuit court of appeals judges, $137,300; associate Supreme Court justices, $159,000; and chief justice, $166,200.[78] During the time span from 1989 to 1991, the median household income for Americans increased slightly from $28,906 to $30,126, but actually decreased in economic terms because inflation made the 1989 income worth $31,750 in 1991 dollars.[79] Thus the judges managed to move themselves even farther away from the mainstream of American society and even higher into the top percentiles of wage earners. Only 4.4 percent of American households had incomes in excess of $100,000 in 1991, and even fewer had incomes in the $120,000 to $160,000 range enjoyed by federal judges.[80]

Because the judges had been unsuccessful in previous efforts to gain congressional action on salary increases, it is clear that the judges do not control legislative action on their salaries. Their success in 1989 shows that they can attempt to influence and occasionally succeed in influencing Congress on this issue. The case study of judicial salaries does not illustrate judges' control over court administration. Instead, it demonstrates how judges' self-interest concerning particular matters affecting court administration may obscure their perspective and understanding about American society and their own privileged place in that society. If judges are removed from mainstream society, how will they understand the problems that litigants present to them in court, and how will they accurately anticipate the social consequences of their decisions? In addition to this fundamental issue about judges' roles and authoritative behavior that is illuminated by the salary issue, judges' concerns about their salaries have implications for other issues and problems.

Several of the justifications for raising federal judicial salaries provided information for society about governmental actions that were needed or desirable. If the judges' dissatisfaction was regarded as a limited problem that could be completely redressed by merely allocating more money for judicial salaries, then the larger policy implications of the compensation issue would be lost. For example, as a reinforcing justification for pay raises, federal judges argued that they were currently doing more work for less pay. Because the real value of judicial salaries declined while case filings simultaneously rose, the judges asserted that they were working within an increasingly pressured environment and deserved increased compensation for their additional responsibilities.[81] Throwing a little extra money in the direction of the judges might have increased their morale, but it was not going to expand their finite abilities for processing the increasing caseload. The real solution involved increasing the resources of the court system in general, by creating new judgeships or by developing alternatives to traditional litigation, as set forth in the provisions of the later Judicial Improvements Act of 1990.

The primary, unrecognized problem underlying judicial dissatisfaction with salaries was not the remediable issue of inflation, but the use of the highly paid elite private bar as a reference group. In addition to losing any recognition of how high their salaries were in relation to the rest of society, judges placed themselves in the undesirable position of being perpetually dissatisfied with their salaries. Judicial salaries can never be expected to approach the astronomical salaries of partners in major law firms, which, according to the figure cited most frequently by federal judges as their reference point, was about $340,000 annually for the top 10 percent of law partners with twenty-five years' experience in cities of 1 million or more people.[82] Thus, even when they gained the raises that they sought, the judges' expectation gap between actual compensation and reference-group salaries remained an insurmountable problem that will continue to undermine judges' perceptions of their professional rewards and perpetuate the salary dissatisfaction that has plagued federal judges for decades.[83]

In discussing the related problems created by excessively inflated salaries for corporate executives, lawyers, and doctors, former Harvard President Derek Bok has proposed an increase in progressive income tax rates. According to Bok, "progressive taxation emerges as a necessary step in any serious effort to limit excessive earnings."[84] Although this mechanism, if appropriately applied to elite lawyers' incomes, could have the beneficial consequence of diminishing federal judges' sense of relative deprivation by reducing high-paid lawyers' actual incomes, the judges would not and could not use their political influence and lobbying efforts to seek such a policy.

As illustrated by Bok's argument, such taxation policies would have broad effects on people throughout society, including judicial officers. However, federal judges, with their elite backgrounds and ties to the legal profession, would never label such a policy as relevant to judicial administration and therefore eligible for attention through the application of judges' political resources and policy-shaping energies. In order to maintain their image and legitimacy as judicial officers, judges must avoid visible involvement in legislative decisions about highly controversial issues, such as tax policy. Judges reserve their political resources and attention for issues that are recognized as directly affecting the courts and thereby inevitably apply their lobbying efforts, whether visible or not, to issues that affect their self-interest, autonomy, authority, status, and accoutrements of judicial office.

Clearly, judges' salaries are an issue of concern for judicial administration. If judges' salaries are too low, the court system will be affected through difficulties with the recruitment of judges. In a worst case scenario, unconscionably low salaries may invite bribery and corruption. People who are concerned about the effective administration of justice, including judges, have good reasons for paying attention to the issue of judicial salaries. Thus, not surprisingly, the federal judges had a basis for casting their arguments about salary increases in terms of preventing adverse consequences for the federal courts. Although the judges could legitimately make arguments based on institutional concerns, they manifested a discernible inability to assess accurately the effects of judicial salaries on the federal courts. As evidenced by the judges' arguments and evidence (or lack thereof) for salary increases, the judges' personal self-interest took precedence over the advancement of institutional interests even though the judges portrayed the issue as creating an imminent threat to the quality of the judiciary.

NOTES

1. Linda Greenhouse, "Rehnquist, in Rare Plea, Asks Raise for Judges," *New York Times*, 16 March 1989, 1.

2. *Statement of Chief Justice William H. Rehnquist* (15 March 1989) (Press release provided by the Administrative Office of the U.S. Courts on behalf of the Judicial Conference of the United States).

3. Committee on the Judicial Branch of the Judicial Conference of the United States, *Simple Fairness: The Case for Equitable Compensation of the Nation's Federal Judges* (Washington, D.C.: Administrative Office of the U.S. Courts, 1988).

4. Federal Salary Act of 1967, codified as amended at 2 U.S.C. § 352–359 (1982 & Supp. V 1987).

5. 2 U.S.C. § 352 (1982).

6. In the aftermath of the Supreme Court's decision in *Immigration and Naturalization Service v. Chadha*, 462 U.S. 919 (1985), which abolished the practice of legislative vetoes by one house of Congress, the Federal Salary Act was amended to provide for rejection of salary recommendations via a joint resolution passed by Congress and signed by the president.

7. Committee on the Judicial Branch, 4–15.

8. For example, Canons 5 and 6 of the ABA Code of Judicial Conduct (1983) prescribe strict limitations on judges' outside financial activities as well as reporting requirements concerning such activities.

9. Richard Posner, *The Federal Courts: Crisis and Reform* (Cambridge: Harvard University Press, 1985), 345–350.

10. Emily Field Van Tassel, *Why Judges Resign: Influences on Federal Judicial Service, 1798 to 1992* (Washington, D.C.: Federal Judicial Center, 1993), 15.

11. Atkins v. United States, 556 F.2d 1028 (Ct. Cl. 1977), *cert.* denied, 434 U.S. 1009 (1978).

12. Remarks of Chief Justice William Rehnquist Before the House Post Office and Civil Service Committee (3 May 1989), 4 (Press release provided by the Administrative Office of the U.S. Courts).

13. Committee on the Judicial Branch, 47, Chart E.

14. Ibid., 46, Chart D.

15. Ibid., 51–52, Chart G.

16. Atkins v. United States, 556 F.2d at 1028.

17. Keith S. Rosenn, "The Constitutional Guaranty Against Diminution of Judicial Compensation," *U.C.L.A. Law Review* 24 (1976): 312–318.

18. Ibid., 350, Table XIII.

19. Committee on the Judicial Branch, 64.

20. Bureau of the Census, *Money Income of Households, Families, and Persons in the United States: 1988 and 1989*, Current Population Reports, Series P-60, No. 172 (Washington, D.C.: Government Printing Office, 1991), 3.

21. Robert Carp and Russell Wheeler, "Sink or Swim: The Socialization of a Federal District Judge," *Journal of Public Law* 21 (1972): 359.

22. Committee on the Judicial Branch, Appendix 2.

23. Ibid., 35.

24. Emily Field Van Tassel, "Why Federal Judges Resign," *Court Historian* 6 (April 1993): 3.

25. Bureau of the Census, *Money Income of Households, Families, and Persons in the United States: 1986*, Current Population Reports, Series P-60, No. 159 (Washington, D..C.: Government Printing Office, 1988), 75.

26. Committee on the Judicial Branch, 34.

27. Posner, 33–34.

28. Van Tassel, *Why Judges Resign*, 15.

29. Press Conference of William H. Rehnquist, Washington, D.C. (15 March 1989) (audio tape of C-SPAN broadcast).

30. Posner, 39.

31. Ibid.

32. Committee on the Judicial Branch, 37.

33. See Charles Percy, "No Royal Road to Justice," *Judicature* 60 (1976): 185.

34. Committee on the Judicial Branch, 24.

35. Posner, 40.

36. Ibid., 42.

37. Paul E. Greenberg and James A. Haley, "The Role of the Compensation Structure in Enhancing Judicial Quality," *Journal of Legal Studies* 15 (1986): 422–426.

38. Posner, 40.

39. Lawrence Baum, *The Supreme Court*, 3d ed. (Washington, D.C.: Congressional Quarterly Press, 1989), 32.

40. Harry P. Stumpf, *American Judicial Politics* (San Diego, Calif.: Harcourt Brace Jovanovich, 1988), 208.

41. Posner, 40.

42. Ibid., 41–43.

43. Richard Kluger, *Simple Justice* (New York: Random House, 1975), 528.

44. Baum, 37.

45. Committee on the Judicial Branch, 63–78.

46. Ibid., 64, Table 14.

47. Bureau of Labor Statistics, *U.S. Department of State Indexes of Living Costs Abroad, Quarters Allowances, and Hardship Differentials* (Washington, D.C.: Government Printing Office, July 1985), 2, 5.

48. Joseph Pechman, ed., *Comparative Tax Systems: Europe, Canada, and Japan* (Arlington, Va.: Tax Analysts, 1987), 32.

49. Committee on the Judicial Branch, 66, Table 15.

50. After *Garcia v. San Antonio Metropolitan Transit Authority*, 469 U.S. 528 (1985), states must, of course, at least meet minimum federal statutory requirements in compensating public employees.

51. Committee on the Judicial Branch, 76, Table 16.

52. "High Education Goals: Low Salary Increases," *Academe* 75 (March–April 1989): 6.

53. Rosenn, 318.

54. Remarks of Chief Justice William Rehnquist, 4–5.

55. Committee on the Judicial Branch, 72 n.45.

56. Remarks of Chief Justice William Rehnquist, 11.

57. Committee on the Judicial Branch, 31.

58. Extrapolating from wage figures for full-time workers, the median annual wage for American workers was $20,384 (i.e., the median weekly earnings during the final quarter of 1988 ($392) multiplied by 52 weeks). Bureau of Labor Statistics, *News Bulletin* (31 January 1989), Table 1.

59. Press Conference of William H. Rehnquist, Washington, D.C. (15 March 1989) (audiotape of C–SPAN broadcast).

60. Committee on the Judicial Branch, 59.

61. Ibid., 61.

62. Ibid., 60.

63. Bureau of the Census, *Money Income of Households, 1988 and 1989*, 19.

64. "Souter and Thomas Report Least Assets of All Justices," *New York Times*, 17 May 1992, 18.

65. "Net Value of Judges' Holdings," *Akron Beacon Journal*, 5 June 1989, C1, C2.

66. Ibid.

67. Committee on the Judicial Branch, 14, Table 5.

68. Albert R. Karr, "House Votes Major Increase in Hourly Wage," *Wall Street Journal*, 24 March 1989, A3.

69. Charles Green, "House Ignores Bush, Votes Pay Level at $4.55," *Akron Beacon Journal*, 24 March 1989, A6.

70. Jeffrey Segal and Harold Spaeth, *The Supreme Court and the Attitudinal Model* (Cambridge: Cambridge University Press, 1993); James L. Gibson, "From Simplicity to Complexity: The Development of Theory in the Study of Judicial Behavior," *Political Behavior* 5 (1983): 7–49; C. Neal Tate, "Personal Attribute Models of the Voting Behavior of U.S. Supreme Court Justices: Liberalism in Civil Liberties and Economics Decisions, 1946–1978," *American Political Science Review* 75 (1981): 355–367.

71. See Christopher E. Smith, *Courts and the Poor* (Chicago: Nelson-Hall, 1991); Kristin Bumiller, *The Civil Rights Society: The Social Construction of Victims* (Baltimore: Johns Hopkins University Press, 1988); Jerold Auerbach, *Unequal Justice: Lawyers and Social Change in Modern America* (New York: Oxford University Press, 1976).

72. United States v. Kras, 409 U.S. 434 (1973).

73. Ortwein v. Schwab, 410 U.S. 656 (1973).

74. Remarks of William H. Rehnquist (Speech at Louisiana State University, Baton Rouge, 11 March 1983), quoted in Lois Forer, *Money and Justice: Who Owns the Courts?* (New York: W. W. Norton, 1984), 77.

75. Judges do not focus on the elite bar as a reference group solely because of financial aspirations. Lawyers in elite law firms also enjoy prestige, influence, and important cases—characteristics that would attract the successful people who compose the federal judiciary. According to one author, "[t]he elite lawyers in the larger firms had the highest income, represented the highest-status clients, and had the most contacts with higher levels of government and the judiciary, compared to those in small firms and individual practitioners." Jerome Corsi, *Judicial Process: An Introduction* (Englewood Cliffs, N.J.: Prentice-Hall, 1984), 66.

76. Katherine S. Mangan, "Law Schools Expect a Record Number of Applicants, but Interest in Public-Service Jobs May Be Waning," *Chronicle of Higher Education*, 1 February 1989, A27.

77. Stephen L. Wasby, *The Supreme Court in the Federal Judicial System*, 4th ed. (Chicago: Nelson-Hall, 1993), 90.

78. Ibid.

79. Bureau of the Census, *Money Income of Households, Families, and Persons in the United States: 1991*, Current Population Reports, Series P-60, No. 180 (Washington, D.C.: Government Printing Office, 1991), xi.

80. Ibid., 9.

81. Committee on the Judicial Branch, 16–20; Thomas Marvell, "Judicial Salaries: Doing More Work for Less Pay," *Judges' Journal* 24 (Winter 1985): 34.

82. Ibid., 71–72.

83. As previously noted, Judge Posner has traced "concerted expression[s] of dissatisfaction with federal judicial salaries" back to 1926. Posner, 33.

84. Derek Bok, *The Cost of Talent: How Executives and Professionals Are Paid and How It Affects America* (New York: Free Press, 1993), 279.

4

Human Consequences: Habeas Corpus Reform

Judges' authority to make decisions in legal cases provides a means through which they can change court procedures. Although judges may genuinely believe that they are advancing the most beneficial policy objectives for the judicial system and society, they cannot always recognize and monitor the element of self-interest that frequently shapes human decision making. As illustrated by this chapter, several Rehnquist Court justices have made efforts to reform habeas corpus procedures in order to advance the goal of limiting the federal courts' caseload. The judicial authority to make case decisions affecting court administration need not have a firm basis in either constitutional or statutory interpretation because judges may simply assert inherent judicial authority to reshape court procedures as long as Congress takes no steps to counteract such activities.

Ten amendments, known as the Bill of Rights, were added to the United States Constitution in 1791 because many people believed that the original Constitution did not provide sufficient specific protections for the rights of individuals. Although the original Constitution focused almost exclusively on the framers' primary mission—namely, establishing the structure and powers of the branches of government—it did not completely neglect protections for individuals. While Americans frequently regard such rights as freedom of speech, freedom of religion, and equal protection as their most important protections against governmental interference, these protections were added to the original Constitution through the amendment process.

Very few protections for individuals were included in the original Constitution as ratified in 1789. The ones that were included presumably were of great importance to the framers, and perhaps of even greater importance than speech, press, and other rights that were added in 1791 and thereafter. Among the few protections for individuals enshrined in the original Constitution was the "privilege of the Writ of Habeas Corpus."[1] A writ of habeas corpus is, in effect, a petition by an incarcerated or otherwise detained person seeking judicial review of the basis and legality of his or her confinement. Because of their fears that government officials might abuse power by arresting political opponents, the authors of the Constitution sought to ensure that prisoners would have access to judges who could free prisoners upon a finding that their arrest and confinement were unlawful.

By placing the "privilege of the Writ of Habeas Corpus" in the body of the Constitution, the founders ensured that neither Congress nor judges could abolish the opportunity for incarcerated individuals to challenge the legality of their confinement. The formal abolition of the writ of habeas corpus would require an amendment to the Constitution initiated and enacted through the arduous amendment process that requires approval by three-fourths of the states' legislatures or constitutional conventions.[2] As indicated by the discussion in this chapter, the founders could never have anticipated how federal judges would eventually use their interpretive powers to limit habeas corpus actions in a manner that effectively precludes federal judicial review of the convictions of many prisoners, including a few who are probably innocent of the crimes for which they were convicted and punished.

CHANGES IN HABEAS CORPUS

Habeas corpus petitions are governed by federal statutory law originating in 1867 that describes the conditions necessary to gain judicial review as the means to seek release from an unlawful incarceration.[3] For example, prisoners in state custody can only challenge their confinement through the habeas corpus process if they can demonstrate violations of their federal constitutional rights. They must also exhaust all available remedies in the state courts before they are permitted to seek review by a federal judge. A decision by the United States Supreme Court in *Fay v. Noia* (1963) expanded opportunities for prisoners to challenge the bases for their convictions and confinements by interpreting the statutory "exhaustion of remedies" requirement.[4] In an opinion by Justice William Brennan, the Court declared that prisoners could seek federal judicial review of claims that the prisoners had failed to raise during their appeals in the state appellate courts. As a result, as Joseph Hoffmann has noted, "After *Fay*, prisoners were free to file habeas petitions based on 'new law' that did not exist at the time of their trials."[5] The expanded availability of the federal courts to review prisoners' claims was consistent with Justice Brennan's theory that "federal constitutional rights of personal liberty shall not be denied without the fullest opportunity for plenary federal review."[6]

The composition of the Supreme Court changed in the early 1970s as President Richard Nixon had the opportunity to appoint four new justices to the high court.[7] Because President Nixon had effectively used "law and order" themes during his presidential campaign, he was eager to appoint Supreme Court justices who would be less receptive than the Warren Court justices to the claims of constitutional rights violations asserted by criminal defendants and prisoners.[8] By appointing Chief Justice Warren Burger and Justices Harry Blackmun, Lewis Powell, and William Rehnquist, all of whom were more conservative than their predecessors on criminal justice issues, President Nixon succeeded in shifting the Supreme Court's perspective on rights for criminal defendants and convicted offenders.

In a concurring opinion in *Schneckloth v. Bustamonte* (1973),[9] Justice Powell advocated a complete reconsideration of *Fay v. Noia*. He believed that Justice Brennan's *Fay* opinion had improperly broadened habeas corpus actions by permitting consideration of constitutional rights that were defined *after* a defendant's case had been decided. Justice Powell argued that Congress intended for habeas corpus doctrines to give greater consideration and deference to the finality of state court decisions rather than to permit federal judges to freely second-guess the judgments of state judges.[10] A few years later, Justice Powell gained support from a majority of justices for reducing the availability of habeas corpus review. In *Stone v. Powell* (1976), Justice Powell delivered the Court's opinion that federal judges could not review habeas petitions claiming violations of Fourth Amendment search and seizure rights if those claims had already received a "full and fair" hearing in a state court.[11] Justice Powell's opinion effectively preempted many potential Fourth Amendment claims that might have been brought to the federal courts and thereby made state judges the final decision makers for such claims.

Justice Brennan's original opinion in *Fay* expanded the availability of habeas corpus by addressing an issue that was not addressed in the federal statute. Thus Justice Brennan's opinion was based on a degree of interpretive freedom that inherently exists in the judicial authority over statutory interpretation when judges may examine "gray areas" or blank spaces in a statutory enactment. By contrast, Justice Powell's opinion seemed to take the application of judicial authority one step further, albeit in the opposite direction, by clashing with the implicit purpose of the statute.

By its words, the statute provides for federal court review of final state court judgments when an issue exists concerning the violation of constitutional rights:

The Supreme Court, a Justice thereof, a circuit judge, or a district court shall entertain an application for a writ of habeas corpus in behalf of a person in custody pursuant to the judgment of a State court only on the ground that he is in custody in violation of the Constitution or laws or treaties of the United States.[12]

The statute does not exclude any category of constitutional claims from consideration, yet Justice Powell's opinion instantly excluded Fourth

Amendment claims that had been reviewed by state court judges. Because judges in most state courts are elected officials who can lose their positions in the next election if they make politically unpopular decisions,[13] they are less insulated than life-tenured federal judges from popular pressures that might deter recognition of legitimate claims by convicted offenders. The existence and wording of the habeas statute indicate that Congress distrusted the reliability of state court decisions and therefore gave federal judges the authority to review prisoners' constitutional claims. In spite of the apparent intentions of the statute, Justice Powell and a majority of Burger Court justices used their judicial authority, in effect, to create an exception in the federal statute.

What is the source of judicial officers' authority to rewrite statutes contrary to the intentions of Congress? If the definition of the scope of habeas corpus and habeas procedures was based on the interpretation of a constitutional provision, the justices would clearly possess the authority to reshape the law. In the realm of constitutional interpretation, it is generally accepted that the judiciary is the ultimate interpreter of the Constitution's meaning. Thus conservative and liberal justices have seized the opportunity to refine and reverse aggressively those constitutional precedents with which they disagree. By contrast, the appropriate judicial role is undisputed with respect to statutory interpretation: to interpret statutory language in a manner that will effectuate the intentions of the legislators who drafted and enacted the laws.[14] As Lawrence Baum has observed, "In the interpretation of federal statutes, the Supreme Court is legally subordinate to Congress."[15] Thus Supreme Court justices should be deferential to congressional statutory language and intent in deciding cases concerning habeas corpus doctrine.

Although habeas corpus rules are a statutory matter under congressional authority, Supreme Court justices have treated them as if they are matters that, like constitutional interpretation, can change instantly according to the preferences of a majority of justices on the high court. When Justice Brennan expanded the applicability of habeas corpus in *Fay v. Noia*, he used his judicial authority to expand the application of habeas relief and advance his preferred policy for protecting the rights of prisoners. Similarly, when conservative justices with different values began to dominate the Court's composition, they used their authority to restrict habeas corpus and undo the consequences of Justice Brennan's *Fay* opinion. Despite its formal control over habeas corpus, Congress has remained on the sidelines as the justices have shaped and reshaped the availability and applicability of habeas relief. According to Hoffmann:

The post–Civil War history of federal habeas reveals that Congress either has followed the lead of the Supreme Court in defining the scope of federal habeas, or has remained completely silent in the face of the Court's numerous decisions interpreting the [habeas corpus statute]. As a result, the Court has come to view the construction of the [habeas corpus statute] as a subject almost completely within its own domain.[16]

As Congress has failed to react to judicially initiated changes in habeas corpus, the Supreme Court's justices have asserted, in their own words, a "historic willingness to overturn and modify [the Court's] earlier views of the scope of the writ [of habeas corpus], even where statutory language authorizing judicial action has remained unchanged."[17]

It is not surprising that Congress has not reacted to the Supreme Court's revisions of habeas corpus doctrine. Relatively few issues rise on the policy agenda of Congress with sufficient momentum to capture the sustained interest and attention of a large body of legislators who are primarily interested in gaining reelection.[18] Because habeas corpus statutes affect only a relatively small number of politically powerless Americans who have earned their despised status in society (i.e., convicted criminal offenders), there is little reason or incentive for elected members of Congress to spend their limited time, energy, and political resources concerning themselves with procedures for reviewing criminal convictions. Thus, despite an absence of formal authority, federal judicial officers have seized and asserted control over habeas corpus rules and procedures. Judicial officers have used their personal policy preferences to expand the scope of habeas corpus, as in Justice Brennan's *Fay* opinion, and to restrict the availability of habeas relief, as in Justice Powell's *Stone* opinion. Although the issue of habeas corpus may appear to involve philosophical disagreements, rather than obvious manifestations of judges' self-interest, habeas corpus developments during the Rehnquist Court era advanced federal judicial officers' perceived self-interest while coinciding with the conservative preferences of the Supreme Court's dominant majority.

THE REHNQUIST COURT AND JUDICIAL SELF-INTEREST

The changing composition of the United States Supreme Court during the 1980s and 1990s generated significant alterations in the high court's decisions. Because the Reagan and Bush administrations made concerted efforts to select justices who would advance politically conservative decisions, the balance of power on the Supreme Court shifted in favor of conservative justices. According to Sheldon Goldman, the Reagan administration "engaged in the most systematic ideological or judicial philosophical screening of judicial candidates since the first Roosevelt administration."[19] President Ronald Reagan and his advisors used this thorough screening to appoint three new justices to the Court, Sandra Day O'Connor, Antonin Scalia, and Anthony Kennedy, and to elevate the Court's most conservative incumbent, William Rehnquist, to chief justice.

The Bush administration emulated the Reagan administration's careful attention to the conservative credentials and beliefs of judicial nominees.[20] By 1992, the Court's composition of eight Republicans and one Democrat was highly unrepresentative of the partisan orientation of the nation as a whole. However, because the Court's composition is determined by the quirks of history concerning which justices die or retire while particular presidents occupy the White House, recent Republican presidents succeeded in cementing a solid conservative majority on the nation's highest court.

The underlying purpose of Presidents Reagan and Bush and their political supporters in seeking to appoint conservative justices to the Supreme Court was to undo the objectionable decisions by the Warren and Burger Courts that established and protected such liberal judicial policies as abortion, affirmative action, school desegregation, and criminal defendants' rights. Although the Rehnquist Court did not initiate complete reversals of precedent for most civil rights and liberties issues,[21] its decisions produced significant reductions in the scope of rights for criminal defendants.[22]

One persistent theme for conservative justices during the Rehnquist Court era was the desire to limit opportunities for convicted offenders to file multiple petitions in the federal courts to seek review of their convictions. According to the correspondent who covered the Court for the *Los Angeles Times*,

Rehnquist was determined to change the [habeas corpus] system. It was chaotic, wasteful, and an abuse of the people's right to have laws enforced, he contended in a series of speeches. . . . Rehnquist was especially upset by inmates who strung out their cases by filing one habeas corpus petition after another. He wanted the law changed to give these inmates a one-time shot.[23]

In the case of prisoners on death row, the habeas process contributes to delays in carrying out convicted murderers' executions. The conservative justices had several reasons for seeking to reform habeas corpus, including their desire to reduce the role of federal courts in supervising state criminal justice systems, to elevate the importance and finality of state courts' decisions, and to enable states to carry out the death penalty expeditiously.[24] Prior to her appointment to the Supreme Court, for example, state judge Sandra Day O'Connor published an article that criticized habeas petitions for causing a burden of duplicative effort by requiring federal courts to review cases already decided by the state courts.[25]

As indicated by Chief Justice Rehnquist's statement in his annual report on the federal judiciary, these justices also manifested self-interest in their desire to reduce the caseload burden on the federal judiciary. This element of self-interest lurked beneath Chief Justice Rehnquist's diplomatic declaration that "[s]tatutory habeas corpus procedures, particularly those dealing with capital cases, are . . . an area where careful reform can preserve the benefits of the Great Writ while rationalizing its application and *eliminating repetitive and time-intensive demands on the federal courts*" (emphasis supplied).[26] Chief Justice Rehnquist's orientation toward limiting the burden of habeas cases was consistent with the actions of "Chief Justice Warren Burger [who] expressed genuine concern about the efficient administration of justice, and [had] his annual reports on the state of the federal judiciary typically includ[e] calls for some limit on habeas as a docket-control measure."[27]

The actual reforms initiated by the justices sought to advance the federal judiciary's self-interest in reducing the federal courts caseload while actually eliminating "the benefits of the Great Writ" for many prisoners despite Chief Justice Rehnquist's professed intentions to the contrary. Not all of the Supreme Court's justices shared the conservatives' self-interested concerns about reducing the burdens on the federal courts. However, a majority of justices pursued their goal of reducing habeas cases by asserting judicial prerogatives, lobbying Congress, and making new judicial decisions.

Federal judges' perceptions about the problems of habeas corpus cases are one component of larger concerns about steadily increasing numbers of cases filed in the federal courts. For example, the number of appeals filed in the federal courts increased by more than 40 percent during the 1980s alone.[28] Caseload pressures felt by federal judges have been exacerbated by a number of factors, including congressional creation of new causes of action and new federal crimes and a dramatic increase in state incarceration rates, meaning more prisoners who can file habeas petitions in the federal courts. Federal judges do not all agree on how to treat the caseload "crisis." They also do not agree on whether or not concerns about court efficiency should take precedence over open access to the courts for litigants and other policy values. However, because a majority of Rehnquist Court justices share grave concerns about caseload burdens, these justices can use their power to advance their view of the judiciary's interest in reducing the number of cases to be decided. These justices undoubtedly see themselves as protecting the judicial branch rather than acting in a self-interested manner, despite the fact that emphasizing caseload concerns over other values also directly advances their own perceived interests as overburdened federal judicial officers.

The source of the self-interest detectable in judicially initiated habeas corpus reform was most clearly enunciated by Justice Scalia. In his first major address to the American Bar Association after being appointed to the Supreme Court, Justice Scalia expressed concern about the "continuing deterioration" of the prestige of the federal courts.[29] Scalia described his aspirations as a law student to become a federal judge because the federal courts were the "forums for the big case."[30] According to Justice Scalia, the framers of the Constitution intended for the federal judiciary to be a "natural aristocracy . . . of ability rather than wealth,"[31] but the federal courts have lost their elite status because they are overloaded with too many cases, including routine cases that do not need to be heard by federal judges. Justice Scalia said that appointing additional judges to handle the caseload would not solve the problem because an increase in the number of federal judges merely dilutes the prestige of judicial office and "aggravates the problem of [maintaining the courts' elite] image."[32] Justice Scalia also rejected the idea of an "Intercircuit Tribunal," a new appellate court below the Supreme Court, because he believed such a new court would "only exacerbate the systemic problems I have been discussing."[33] Because, Justice Scalia "wanted to be a judge, not a case processor,"[34] he proposed the creation of specialized courts "for large categories of high-volume, relatively routine cases—Social Security disability cases, for example, and freedom of information actions—to be disposed of with finality before an administrative law judge [ALJ], providing appeal to the courts on issues of law only if the ALJ's decision is reversed by the agency."[35]

Although Justice Scalia did not say so explicitly, prisoners' cases are widely regarded by federal judges as another category of burdensome, routine, and repetitive cases. One of the catalysts for the creation of the U.S. magistrates in 1968 was complaints to Congress that, in the words of one judge's congressional testimony, prisoners' cases "take up an inordinate amount of time."[36] One study found that federal district judges "tend to regard [habeas corpus cases] as weary, stale, flat, and unprofitable."[37] Because prisoners have no right to representation by counsel for habeas corpus petitions, many petitions are presented *pro se*, with the prisoners attempting to put forward their own constitutional claims. Many prisoners have little education, difficulty with the English language, and literacy problems, and, therefore, they cannot effectively present coherent arguments.[38] Such petitions become even more burdensome to judicial personnel because they are so difficult to decipher. As a result, many prisoners' cases are delegated to inexperienced law clerks who, in the course of applying routinized decision making to such cases, may look first for reasons to dismiss the cases rather than examine the petitions to see if they present genuine constitutional issues.[39]

Prison populations continued to grow in the 1980s and 1990s. Figures from the Bureau of Justice Statistics show that "[t]here were only 329,821 people in prison in 1980, but that number leaped to 771,243 in 1990 as a result of aggressive prosecutions and stiffer sentences for narcotics and other offenses."[40] Thus increasing incarceration rates throughout the country threatened the federal judiciary with natural and inevitable increases in these undesirable and routine petitions from prisoners. In 1993, habeas petitions constituted only 6 percent of the 276,000 cases filed in the federal district courts. However, the numbers of habeas petitions increased between 1992 and 1993 while civil and criminal case filings generally declined slightly.[41] Fundamentally, many federal judicial officers view the growing habeas caseload as unnecessarily burdensome.

Because habeas corpus procedures are governed by statutes, rather than by the United States Constitution, Congress should control prisoners' access to the federal courts for collateral review of alleged federal constitutional rights violations in criminal convictions. This does not imply, however, that judges lack a legitimate avenue for seeking to initiate reforms of habeas corpus and other court-related issues. As illustrated by the discussion in Chapter 2, a legislative policy is not immune from the reform initiatives of judges because Congress is receptive to and influenced by judges' suggestions when developing or altering statutes that affect the judiciary. Moreover, "as indicated by studies of judicial lobbying, Congress is especially receptive to communications from judicial officers when the judges appear to speak with a unified voice."[42] Thus, Chief Justice Rehnquist initially set about attempting to reform habeas corpus procedures by urging Congress to enact legislation to diminish opportunities for prisoners to file multiple petitions in the federal courts.

In 1989, Chief Justice Rehnquist appointed retired Justice Powell to head the Ad Hoc Committee on Federal Habeas Corpus in Capital Cases, which was supposed to study and create recommendations for reform of habeas corpus procedures in death penalty cases.[43] Justice Powell's committee presented Chief Justice Rehnquist with a proposal to generally limit death-row inmates to one habeas corpus petition and to impose shorter time limits on the review process:

Under the proposal, if a state provides qualified counsel to handle state post-conviction proceedings in capital cases, then capital defendants in that state would be (1) subjected to a 180–day statute of limitations for filing their federal habeas corpus petitions, with a possible 60–day extension for good cause, (2) limited to one federal habeas corpus petition absent a claim that raises serious doubt about the defendant's guilt, and that was not raised previously because of a valid excuse, such as newly discovered evidence, and (3) prevented from challenging the effectiveness of their state post-conviction attorneys.[44]

Although the proposal was criticized for being unfair to capital defendants by singling out death-row inmates for accelerated procedures, Chief Justice Rehnquist submitted the proposal to the Judicial Conference of the United States to seek the judiciary's endorsement for using the Powell committee's proposal as the basis for new legislation to recommend to Congress. Chief Justice Rehnquist apparently adopted the approach of using Justice Powell and the Judicial Conference to promote habeas corpus reform because "Congress often defers to judges or seeks the Judicial Conference's endorsement when considering court-reform legislation."[45] Thus, for example, "[v]irtually all major legislation affecting the [Supreme]

Court's jurisdiction was drafted by Justices and was the result of their lobbying."[46]

At their September 1989 meeting, the judges on the Judicial Conference decided to defer any decision on the Powell committee's proposals until their March 1990 meeting.[47] The judges wanted to return to their respective circuits to solicit comments and reactions from other judges throughout the country. After the September meeting, Chief Justice Rehnquist submitted the proposals to Congress without waiting for the forthcoming discussion and decision by the Judicial Conference. This eagerness to push forward with habeas corpus reform elicited a nearly unprecedented public rebuke of the chief justice by a majority of judges on the Judicial Conference who sent a letter to Congress disavowing the proposals and informing the legislature that the proposal represented the views of Chief Justice Rehnquist and the Powell committee, but did not represent the views of the entire federal judiciary.[48] At its March meeting, the Judicial Conference ultimately decided to support more modest limitations on habeas corpus than those advanced by Chief Justice Rehnquist and the Powell committee. Although the habeas corpus reform proposal was presented to Congress and the individual houses of Congress passed bills related to such reforms, the combined houses of Congress and President George Bush never reached any agreement on a major crime bill that would include habeas corpus reform.[49]

Chief Justice Rehnquist's lack of success in persuading Congress to alter the habeas corpus statute to limit filings by prisoners did not halt the efforts by him and his conservative colleagues to reform habeas procedures. He used his prerogatives as chief justice to reshuffle the assignments of his colleagues as circuit justices who oversee urgent petitions from the various federal circuit courts of appeals. In 1991, Chief Justice Rehnquist transferred Justice Byron White from his position as circuit justice for the Fifth Circuit and replaced him with Justice Scalia. The Fifth Circuit covers Texas, Louisiana, and Mississippi, states whose active application of the death penalty generates a disproportionate number of habeas corpus petitions from death-row prisoners. Justice Scalia used his discretionary authority as circuit justice to announce immediately that he was changing White's policy of granting extensions to death-row inmates who were not represented by attorneys. He began to apply quite strictly the ninety–day filing deadlines for petitions from death-row inmates, even though many uneducated, indigent prisoners are incapable of discovering and following proper legal procedures and deadlines.[50] In effect, Justice Scalia was able to preclude the filing of many habeas petitions from the Fifth Circuit without seeking the cooperation or approval of Congress, other Supreme Court justices, or anyone else.

In addition to such individual actions to reduce the caseload burden posed by habeas cases, Rehnquist Court justices embarked on an effort to reform through judicial decisions a policy that is governed by the statutes that elected officials in Congress have left intact. Although judicial limitations on habeas corpus began during the Burger Court era with Justice Powell's opinion in *Stone*, a significant acceleration of such decisions occurred during the Rehnquist Court era. In 1989, for example, "Justice O'Connor's lead opinions for a plurality of the Court in *Teague v. Lane*,[51] and for a majority in the followup case of *Penry v. Lynaugh*,[52] significantly narrowed the scope of federal habeas by excluding claims based on 'new constitutional rules of civil procedure,' or rules that are announced after a defendant's conviction becomes 'final.' "[53] These decisions diminished the likelihood that federal courts would accept and view favorably claims from state prisoners:

Teague shifts the focus of federal habeas from the correction of constitutional errors affecting the conviction of an individual defendant to the deterrence . . . of constitutional errors by state courts. . . . The lower federal courts will also be much less likely to find merit in a second or subsequent habeas petition. And the Supreme Court will not review habeas at all [with few exceptions] . . . because, after *Teague*, almost all certiorari petitions filed by state prisoners will be either uncertworthy, because they do not raise novel legal issues, or unreviewable, because they raise issues that cannot be decided in the petitioner's favor.[54]

The conservatives on the Supreme Court moved ahead with their own policy objective of increasing efficiency in the federal courts at the expense of accessible, thorough federal court reviews of criminals' convictions. This judicial activism for the sake of court efficiency required a reduction in the judiciary's responsibility for preventing miscarriages of justice because limitations on reviews increased the likelihood that state courts would make mistakes that would remain uncorrected by federal judges who were previously available to review habeas petitions. According to J. Thomas Sullivan, "[t]he trend in the Court's decisions is to elevate technical performance over substance in the evaluation of claims of federal rights violations."[55] This shift in emphasis was consistent with Chief Justice Rehnquist's view that the Supreme Court should not concern itself with correcting injustices. According to Chief Justice Rehnquist, "[t]he Supreme Court of the United States should be reserved . . . for important disputes and questions of law, not for individual injustices that might be corrected and should be corrected in other courts."[56] As indicated by the following specific Supreme Court decisions affecting habeas corpus, this judicial activism in rewriting legal rules supposedly governed by the habeas statute created the risk that the federal courts will turn a blind eye to significant questions of injustice produced by errors in state criminal justice systems.[57]

Butler v. McKellar

Although the Court's decision in *Butler v. McKellar*[58] was an application of the *Teague* and *Penry* decisions limiting federal court review of habeas petitions, rather than the enunciation of a new habeas corpus rule, the case illustrates the risk that decisions intended, in part, to preserve the judiciary's resources will diminish appropriate concerns for correcting injustice.

Horace Butler was convicted and sentenced to death for the brutal rape and murder of a woman in South Carolina after police questioned him in jail where he was being held on unrelated assault charges. Although he was represented by counsel on the assault charges, Butler signed a "waiver of rights" form and was questioned by police outside of the presence of his counsel concerning the murder. The incriminating statements that Butler made to police during the interrogations resulted in his conviction and death sentence for first-degree murder.

Butler challenged his conviction through the habeas corpus process by claiming that the police-initiated interrogation outside of the presence of his counsel violated his rights. On the very same day that the U.S. court of appeals rejected Butler's claim, the United States Supreme Court issued a decision in a separate case declaring that when someone is being held on a criminal charge and is represented by counsel on that charge, police officers may not initiate an interrogation of the suspect concerning separate charges.[59] When Butler subsequently submitted a habeas petition based on the Supreme Court's clear declaration that his rights had been violated by the police interrogation, a five-member majority on the Court decided that a judicially created habeas rule precluded Butler from benefitting from a "new" ruling concerning criminal procedure.[60] The Court's decision acknowledged that the police interrogation conducted in a case identical to Butler's was unconstitutional and therefore impermissible, but the ruling would not be applied retroactively to benefit Butler.

In dissent, Justice Brennan, joined by Justices Thurgood Marshall, John Paul Stevens, and Blackmun, scored the majority for hypocritically usurping the legislative authority of the people's elected representatives in Congress:

It is Congress and not this Court who is "responsible for defining the scope of the writ [of habeas corpus]." Yet the majority, whose Members often pride themselves on their reluctance to play an "activist" judicial role by infringing on legislative prerogatives, does not hesitate today to dismantle Congress' extension of federal habeas corpus to state prisoners.[61]

As is true of many Supreme Court cases, the details of the lives of individual participants in cases can be obscured by courtroom battles and judges' decisions concerning narrow issues of law.[62] In the case of Horace Butler, the human details reveal that the justices' self-interested judicial activism in habeas corpus reform created the risk that an innocent man would face execution by the state of South Carolina.

According to a *Washington Post* investigation, Butler is a mentally retarded man with an IQ of 61, which leads him to have the mental functioning of a nine-year-old.[63] Butler entered first grade when he was 12 years old and dropped out of third grade four years later. These facts alone call into question whether Butler was competent to waive his right to the presence of his attorney during an all-night, jailhouse interrogation session initiated by the police. The prosecutor in the case later said that he never would have sought the death penalty if he had known that Butler was mentally retarded, but Butler's inexperienced attorney never had his client tested and never presented any evidence about Butler's mental capacity to the court. The jury that convicted Butler and sentenced him to death was also never told about his clean criminal record. Although most defense attorneys would charge tens of thousands of dollars to handle a capital murder case,[64] indigent defendant Butler was deprived of his opportunity to have an experienced death-penalty attorney as his court-appointed counsel when his well-intentioned family found a "bumbling defense lawyer who was paid just $300 and who spent a mere 10 minutes giving the jury evidence of why his client should not be put to death."[65] In addition to these questions about the reliability of Butler's confession and the effectiveness of his defense representation, "an FBI agent testified that a . . . pubic hair found on [the rape-murder victim's] blouse was definitely not from Butler."[66]

The end result of the case was that the Supreme Court acknowledged that Butler's rights were violated by the police-initiated interrogation, yet the justices' desire to reduce opportunities for habeas petitions in the federal courts meant that Butler had no opportunity to have a federal court vindicate his rights. Butler had little understanding of what happened to him.

Butler, who has complained of hearing voices and has been involuntarily committed to state psychiatric facilities five times while in prison, seems to have little grasp of his case. Polite and passive, he could not name the president of the United States or explain the meaning of mentally retarded. Told that mentally retarded people found it harder than others to learn, Butler . . . says: "So if I finish high school, I wouldn't be retarded?"[67]

Despite his diminished mental capacity, he faced execution for a crime that he may not have committed as the result of police interrogation that the Supreme Court's justices acknowledge violated his rights.

McCleskey v. Zant

Warren McCleskey, an African-American man, was convicted and sentenced to death in Georgia for killing a white police officer during a furniture store robbery. McCleskey's case first reached the United States

Supreme Court in 1987 when he presented powerful statistical evidence that African-American defendants, especially those convicted of killing whites, received death sentences for racially biased reasons.[68] Scholars conducted a statistical analysis of 2,000 murder cases in Georgia that showed "[t]he disproportionate sentences could be explained only by the presence of racial discrimination because the researchers [controlled for the effects of] 230 potentially explanatory variables in[] their study."[69] Despite showing that "defendants charged with killing white victims were 4.3 times as likely to receive a death sentence as defendants charged with killing blacks,"[70] a five-member majority on the Supreme Court rejected the use of statistical evidence as a basis for showing the existence of improper discrimination in capital sentencing.

After his first loss in the Supreme Court, McCleskey filed a second habeas petition in 1987, which led to a second argument before the Supreme Court.[71] In 1987, McCleskey's attorney learned that the man placed in McCleskey's jail cell with him after his murder arrest in 1978 was an informer working for the police who subsequently testified that McCleskey made incriminating statements in the cell.[72] Because McCleskey had asserted his right to counsel at that time, the police were not permitted to question him or to have anyone else question him outside the presence of counsel. Thus the actions taken by the police constituted a basis to assert a violation of McCleskey's right under *Massiah v. United States* to have his attorney present during any questioning by police or their agents.[73]

A six-member majority on the Supreme Court rejected McCleskey's second habeas petition by declaring that McCleskey should have asserted all of his claims in his first habeas petition filed in 1981,[74] despite McCleskey's claim that his cellmate's status as a police informer in violation of established *Massiah* principles was hidden from his attorney until 1987. According to the petitioner, by improperly hiding the evidence of their own misconduct, the police and prosecutors prevented McCleskey from having his case thoroughly reviewed by a federal judge.

As summarized by one commentator, the conservative majority had further redefined habeas corpus procedures so that "[a]ll such claims must be filed immediately after the conviction. . . . The courthouse door would now be closed to a second habeas corpus petition, except in those rare instances where inmates have strong evidence that they are innocent."[75] Although McCleskey was not presenting strong evidence that he was innocent in raising his *Massiah* claim, he mounted a plausible challenge to the strength of the prosecution's case against him. If McCleskey's attorneys had known that the cellmate was a police informant at the time of the original trial, they could have informed the jury to be on guard against self-serving testimony by a criminal defendant seeking to curry favor with law enforcement authorities by testifying against McCleskey.

Whether or not the jurors would have discounted the informer's testimony as self-interested and thereby changed their decision about McCleskey's guilt will never be known. Because "no one witnessed the shooting,"[76] McCleskey's first-degree murder conviction was based primarily on circumstantial evidence and self-interested testimony by one of McCleskey's accomplices and by the cellmate. Without the self-serving testimony of the two criminal defendants (i.e., the accomplice and the cellmate) seeking to gain favor with the police by testifying against McCleskey, there is no basis for knowing whether it was McCleskey or one of his three accomplices who actually shot the police officer during the robbery. Despite the apparent question about whether McCleskey was in fact the murderer, he was the one convicted of murder and, after the Supreme Court rejected his second habeas petition despite the showing that his *Massiah* rights had been violated, he was the one executed for the killing of the police officer.

Not surprisingly, Justice Marshall, joined by Justices Stevens and Blackmun, issued a vigorous dissent that castigated the activist conservative justices for rewriting habeas corpus procedures that are supposed to be under the authority of Congress rather than the courts:

Ironically, the majority seeks to defend its doctrinal innovation on the ground that it will promote respect for the "rule of law." . . . Obviously, respect for the rule of law must start with those who are responsible for *pronouncing* the law. The majority's invocation of "the orderly administration of justice" . . . rings hollow when the majority itself tosses aside established precedents without explanation, disregards the will of Congress, fashions rules that defy the reasonable expectations of the persons who must conform their conduct to the law's dictates, and applies those rules in a way that rewards state misconduct and deceit.[77]

Coleman v. Thompson

Roger Coleman was convicted of raping and murdering a woman in a small Virginia coal mining town. He was sentenced to death for these crimes. After losing his appeal in the Virginia Supreme Court, he filed an unsuccessful habeas petition in the Virginia state courts.[78] His lawyers subsequently sought to file a habeas corpus petition in the federal courts, but they made an error in missing a filing deadline. Virginia procedural rules require that legal papers be filed at the court within thirty days after a judge issues a final judgment.[79] In Coleman's case, however, "[s]ome 29 days after a court clerk had stamped his conviction final, his lawyer filed [the federal habeas petition]. Actually, this filing . . . came 33 days after the judge had signed an order making the conviction final."[80] Coleman's attorneys had relied on the court clerk's erroneous date stamp on the judicial order. Although they had reason to believe that they were filing in a timely fashion, they actually filed a few days late. The United States Supreme

Court responded to Coleman's case by creating a new habeas corpus rule declaring that any violations of state court procedures forfeit a claimant's opportunity to obtain federal court review of alleged constitutional violations.[81] Thus the error by Coleman's attorney in mistakenly filing the petition three days late prevented any federal judge from considering whether Coleman's conviction was valid.

As an assertion of the conservative justices' preference for efficiency over considerations of remedying injustice, this judicially altered habeas corpus rule has especially significant effects on poor litigants who rely on court-appointed counsel at trial and who have no right to court-appointed counsel in later initiating habeas proceedings.[82] There is a substantial academic literature that raises questions about whether less affluent defendants receive competent, zealous representation from court-appointed attorneys. Studies indicate that there is a significant risk that the attorneys' interests in disposing of cases quickly will diminish the quality of representation afforded to such defendants.[83] In capital cases, some state judges avoid the risk of electoral damage from presiding over the acquittal of a murder defendant by ensuring that the best attorneys are not appointed to represent indigent capital defendants.[84] Moreover, the risks of inadequate judicial detection of trial courts' errors are compounded by rigid habeas rules that lead to forfeiture of claims for prisoners, many of whom have low IQs, minimal education, little knowledge of legal procedures, and inadequate command of the English language, who must attempt to draft and file their own petitions in court without the assistance of attorneys.

In a dissenting opinion, Justice Blackmun, joined by Justices Stevens and Marshall, criticized the majority for "creating a Byzantine morass of arbitrary, unnecessary, and unjustifiable impediments to the vindication of federal rights."[85] Justice Blackmun also complained about the majority's preoccupation with scarce judicial resources and other priorities at the expense of considerations of justice:

Federalism; comity; state sovereignty; preservation of state resources; certainty; the majority methodically inventories these multifarious state interests. . . . One searches the majority's opinion in vain, however, for any mention of petitioner Coleman's right to a criminal proceeding free from constitutional defect. . . .[86]

As in other cases that have been blocked from review by the conservative justices' efforts to rewrite habeas corpus procedures, questions remain about the evidence that led to Coleman's conviction and, ultimately, to his execution—questions that could not be examined by the federal courts because, under the Supreme Court's ruling, the filing error by Coleman's lawyer made them unreviewable. According to an investigative report by *Time* magazine, Coleman was represented by an inexperienced and admittedly reluctant court-appointed attorney who was only two years out of law school and had only handled one murder case before.[87] The case against Coleman was built solely around circumstantial evidence and questionable physical evidence because there were no witnesses, fingerprints, murder weapons, or motives that the prosecution could link to Coleman.[88] Coleman had six alibi witnesses who could account for all of his movements on the night of the murder except for a thirty-minute period during which, the prosecution theorized, "Coleman parked his truck, waded across a creek, climbed a hill the length of three football fields, raped [the victim] twice, slit her throat, and escaped unseen."[89] Although there was some evidence of water and blood on Coleman's clothes, the amounts were less than one would expect to be on the killer.[90] A neighbor of the victim found bloody shirts and sheets that were apparently abandoned by someone other than Coleman, but Coleman's attorney never presented this evidence. The blood sample used as evidence against Coleman fit the blood type of roughly 10 percent of the population, and a fingerprint found at the scene was never connected to Coleman. The jailhouse informer who testified against Coleman was released after testifying, and one of the informer's relatives claimed that the informer later admitted that he manufactured the testimony.[91]

In addition, there were other questions raised about the reliability of Coleman's conviction:

In late 1991 [a town resident] signed an affidavit swearing that another man in the county had confessed to [the] murder [for which Coleman was convicted]. . . . [Later] four more witnesses came forward, all with stories pointing to the same man. . . . The jailhouse snitch's version of Coleman's "confession" put another man on the murder scene. . . . [T]he police deputy who had been assigned to trail Coleman right after the murder, swore . . . in an affidavit, "I believe that the principal reason for Mr. Coleman's arrest and trial was to reassure the community that a perpetrator had been found." [The deputy] was never summoned as a defense witness.[92]

Despite these questions about Coleman's guilt, he was sentenced to death and executed, in part, because he was a poor defendant whose inexperienced court-appointed attorney made errors in representing him. With the creation of new barriers to habeas corpus review in the federal courts, there are risks that other "Colemans" will be blocked from the federal court system by the justices' alterations of habeas corpus procedures.[93]

JUDICIAL SELF-INTEREST AND THE INTERESTS OF JUSTICE

As a result of the Rehnquist Court justices' decisions, there are risks that the growing limitations on habeas corpus will prevent federal judges from discovering miscarriages of justice. Individual prisoners have emerged who possess powerful evidence of their innocence, yet remain blocked from habeas relief.[94] The questions about one such prisoner's innocence were so strong that even the author of *Coleman v. Thompson*, Justice O'Connor, dissented from the Court's denial of the prisoner's petition to have his case heard. The prisoner's case was barred under the doctrine created by O'Connor's opinion in *Coleman v. Thompson* because his lawyer violated a state procedural rule by filing the wrong document. Thus, due to a lawyer's error, the prisoner may never receive federal court review of his case, which involves strong indications of his innocence:

> Mr. O'Dell was convicted of murdering a woman at Virginia Beach. Both had spent part of the evening at the same bar, although there was no evidence that they had been there together or that they knew each other. The evidence that led to his conviction was circumstantial, based largely on a chemical test indicating that blood on his clothes matched the victim's blood.
>
> After his conviction, a new type of blood analysis came into use. Using this more sophisticated test, based on DNA, the two blood samples did not match, but the state courts did not permit him to introduce the new evidence. Mr. O'Dell's lawyers are also challenging the trial court's ruling that permitted him to represent himself, despite a previous diagnosis of paranoid schizophrenia.[95]

The justices' preferences for preserving judicial resources, rather than reviewing prisoners' cases, were well illustrated by Justice Scalia's concurring opinion in *Herrera v. Collins* in 1993.[96] The case concerned whether a death-row inmate was entitled to judicial consideration of newly discovered evidence purporting to show that he was actually innocent of the murder for which he was convicted. While the dissenting justices claimed that the execution of an innocent person would violate the Eighth Amendment's prohibition on cruel and unusual punishments, Justice Scalia argued that the Constitution provides no right for an innocent person to avoid being executed after being duly convicted of a capital offense: "There is no basis in text, tradition, or even in contemporary practice (if that were enough), for finding in the Constitution a right to demand judicial reconsideration of newly discovered evidence of innocence brought forward after conviction."[97] In his opinion, Justice Scalia asserted that "newly discovered evidence relevant only to a state prisoner's guilt or innocence is not a basis for federal habeas corpus relief"[98] and thereby sought to reinforce another barrier to habeas petitions. Moreover, Justice Scalia explicitly emphasized his underlying motivation of judicial self-interest:

> My concern is that . . . we not appear to make it harder for the lower federal courts, imposing upon them the burden of regularly analyzing newly-discovered-evidence-of-innocence claims in capital cases (in which event such federal claims, it can confidently be predicted, will become routine and repetitive).[99]

Which is more important to the judicial system, ensuring that innocent people are not wrongly executed for capital offenses or sparing federal judges from the burden of reviewing claims that new evidence of innocence has been discovered? Value choices must inevitably be made when determining how to process cases and how to balance properly the need for efficiency with the demand for reliable decisions. The trend of decisions from the Rehnquist Court's majority clearly evinces a desire to protect the federal judiciary from the burden of prisoners' habeas corpus petitions. As indicated by the foregoing discussion, these justices have pursued their goals by using every means available to them, including lobbying Congress, rigorously enforcing discretionary procedural rules, and revising statutory habeas procedures through new judicial decisions. These justices need not acknowledge that they are placing judicial self-interest above, in some cases, the lives of prisoners who may have been wrongly convicted. Instead, they claim that they are striking the appropriate balance between efficiency and justice by rationalizing to themselves that any actual miscarriages of justice will be corrected through the application of governors' pardon power.[100]

A significant irony lurks beneath the Rehnquist Court's efforts to reduce the burden of habeas corpus cases in the federal courts. Instead of protecting lower court judicial officers and the court system's finite resources, the judicially initiated reform of habeas corpus procedures has apparently actually *increased* the burdens on many district court decision makers. A survey of seventy-four U.S. magistrate judges in the twenty-five district courts with the heaviest habeas caseloads found that only 14 percent of these judicial officers who make the preliminary recommendations in habeas cases believe that the Supreme Court's reform of habeas procedures has reduced their workload.[101]

Moreover, many of the magistrate judges commented that the Supreme Court's reform of procedural issues has actually created more work by giving district court personnel more issues to analyze in each case. For example, one respondent commented that "[p]rocedural bar issues are often more difficult than resolution on the merits would be, so the recent trend expanding rules regarding procedural bar makes deciding [habeas] cases more difficult and time consuming, not less."[102] The emphasis on procedural issues also creates additional work for judicial personnel in examining the procedural issues for each case. According to one respondent, "[a]lthough fewer habeas petitions are reviewed on the merits, our office often must spend substantial amounts of time reviewing confusing procedural histories."[103] In the words of another magistrate judge,

Mandatory procedural compliance prior to any examination of the merits often creates more work. The state must file the entire record of trial and appellate proceedings. The record must be reviewed to see if a weak or frivolous claim has been exhausted. In many cases, it would be easier for all concerned to dismiss on the merits.[104]

The Supreme Court's reforms also slow down the processing of cases by increasing the number of delays as judicial personnel respond to motions from lawyers for the state. As described by one magistrate judge, "Our state [attorney general] responds, raising procedural bar [defenses], but then if we disagree they want more time to respond on the merits, so time is increased, not decreased."[105] There is also a perception that reform of habeas corpus had the unintended consequence of generating *more* civil rights lawsuits by prisoners. According to one respondent, "[t]he perceived threat to the viability of habeas corpus in prisoners' minds has resulted in a significant increase in filing of section 1983 civil rights claims to adjudicate the same issues (e.g., malpractice-type suits [versus] their [public defenders and criminal defense] attorneys) *without* reducing habeas petitions filed."[106] Like other decision makers elsewhere in government, the Supreme Court's justices obviously cannot anticipate the consequences of their decisions, even when those decisions are motivated by self-interest and aimed at a specific category of activities within their own bailiwick.

CONCLUSION

It may be desirable or even necessary to address the perceived problem of overburdened resources in the federal courts. Resource problems can be addressed either through an increase in resources or through a reduction in demands on the system. Federal judges cannot readily initiate the legislative action necessary to increase judicial resources, although Chapter 2 demonstrated how judges can shape such initiatives when judicial resources have already earned a place on the legislative policy agenda. Thus the only mechanism within direct control of the federal judges is their ability to reduce the number of cases presented in the federal courts.

With respect to prisoner litigation, contrary to the impression conveyed by the statements of Chief Justice Rehnquist and other critics of habeas corpus practices, 70 percent of all prisoners' cases in the federal courts are *not* habeas corpus petitions. Instead, they are civil rights lawsuits by prisoners. As Jim Thomas has demonstrated, judges' denigrating characterizations of prisoners' petitions as "overly burdensome" are often based on ideological perceptions and anecdotal evidence rather than on systematic analysis of the substance of prisoners' filings in the federal courts.[107] Indeed, empirical studies of habeas corpus petitions conducted prior to the Rehnquist Court's recent reform initiatives indicated that many of the criticisms leveled at the purportedly abusive practices of habeas petitioners (i.e., failing to exhaust state remedies, failing to file in a timely manner, and filing multiple petitions) are readily explainable and less problematic than typically portrayed.[108]

Federal judges have sought to limit habeas petitions because habeas procedures are most readily within their control. Congress has made little effort to supervise habeas reform, and, therefore, the judges have used their authority to fill the policy vacuum and shape habeas reform. Indeed, disagreements among legislators meant that neither chamber of the national legislature included habeas corpus reform in its versions of the major 1994 crime legislation, and thus the judicial initiatives remained undisturbed.[109] Although prisoners' civil rights lawsuits represent a larger and more burdensome body of cases than do habeas corpus petitions, any judicial reform of civil rights statutes potentially affects civil rights litigation by people throughout society and not just by prisoners. The Rehnquist Court learned in 1991 that Congress is much more likely to react to judicial efforts to reform general civil rights when the Civil Rights Act of 1991 reversed seven Supreme Court decisions that had narrowed the scope of civil rights statutes in 1989.[110] Thus the justices seized control of habeas corpus reform because there were no alternative policy makers actively involved in counteracting or restraining their efforts.

The efforts of the Rehnquist Court majority to reform habeas procedures illustrate the power possessed by federal judicial officers to advance their own perceived interests through their authority to make judicial decisions. The justices who advanced habeas corpus reform undoubtedly see themselves as providing benefits to the judicial system by reducing the number of repetitive, burdensome filings from a class of litigants that is undeserving of any sympathy or extra consideration. In undertaking their efforts to preserve judicial resources, however, the justices' self-interest may have encouraged a degree of myopia. The justices succeeded in limiting some prisoners' access to the courts, but the achievement of that goal simultaneously had destructive impacts on the workload of lower-level judicial officers and the opportunities for federal courts to vindicate the rights of deserving or wrongly convicted prisoners. As indicated by the example of habeas corpus reform, the infusion of self-interest into policy making can reduce the comprehensiveness of policy planning and the ability of policy makers to anticipate accurately the consequences of their decisions.

NOTES

1. U.S. Const., art. I, § 9, cl. 2.

2. Ibid., art. V.

3. 28 U.S.C. §§ 2254–2255.

4. Fay v. Noia, 372 U.S. 391 (1963).

5. Joseph L. Hoffmann, "The Supreme Court's New Vision of Federal Habeas Corpus for State Prisoners," *Supreme Court Review* (1989): 176.

6. Fay v. Noia, 372 U.S. at 424.

7. See Christopher E. Smith, " 'What If. . . .': Critical Junctures on the Road to (In)Equality," *Thurgood Marshall Law Review* 15 (1989–1990): 10–17.

8. Christopher E. Smith, *Justice Antonin Scalia and the Supreme Court's Conservative Moment* (Westport, Conn.: Praeger, 1993), 9–11.

9. Schneckloth v. Bustamonte, 412 U.S. 218 (1973).

10. Ibid., 250 (Powell, J., concurring). See also Yale Kamisar, Wayne R. La-Fave, and Jerold H. Israel, *Modern Criminal Procedure*, 7th ed. (St. Paul, Minn.: West Publishing, 1990), 1523.

11. Stone v. Powell, 428 U.S. 465 (1976).

12. 28 U.S.C. § 2254(a).

13. Christopher E. Smith, *Courts, Politics, and the Judicial Process* (Chicago: Nelson-Hall, 1993), 89–109.

14. William Louthan, *The United States Supreme Court: Lawmaking in the Third Branch of Government* (Englewood Cliffs, N.J.: Prentice-Hall, 1991), 130.

15. Lawrence Baum, *The Supreme Court*, 3d ed. (Washington, D.C.: Congressional Quarterly Press, 1992), 229–230.

16. Hoffmann, 177.

17. Wainwright v. Sykes, 433 U.S. 72, 81 (1977).

18. See John W. Kingdon, *Agendas, Alternatives, and Public Policies* (Boston: Little, Brown, 1984).

19. Sheldon Goldman, "Reagan's Second Term Judicial Appointments: The Battle at Midway," *Judicature* 70 (1987): 326.

20. Neil Lewis, "Bush Picking the Kind of Judges Reagan Favored," *New York Times*, 10 April 1990, A19.

21. See Christopher E. Smith and Thomas R. Hensley, "Assessing the Conservatism of the Rehnquist Court," *Judicature* 77 (1993): 83–89.

22. See John F. Decker, *Revolution to the Right: Criminal Procedure During the Burger-Rehnquist Court Era* (New York: Garland, 1992); Alfredo Garcia, *The Sixth Amendment in Modern Jurisprudence: A Critical Perspective* (New York: Greenwood, 1992).

23. David G. Savage, *Turning Right: The Making of the Rehnquist Court* (New York: John Wiley & Sons, 1992), 412–413.

24. Linda Greenhouse, "A Window on the Court: Justices Take an Assertive Role to Reduce Habeas Corpus Petitions by State Inmates," *New York Times*, 6 May 1992, A1, A20.

25. Sandra Day O'Connor, "Trends in the Relationship Between the Federal and State Courts from the Perspective of a State Court Judge," *William and Mary Law Review* 22 (1981): 801.

26. William H. Rehnquist, "Chief Justice's 1991 Year-End Report on the Federal Judiciary," *The Third Branch* 24 (January 1992): 3.

27. Larry Yackle, "The Habeas Hagioscope," *Southern California Law Review* 66 (1993): 2355.

28. Administrative Office of the U.S. Courts, *Annual Report of the Director of the Administrative Office of the U.S. Courts* (Washington, D.C.: U.S. Government Printing Office, 1989), 2.

29. Stuart Taylor, "Scalia Proposes Major Overhaul of U.S. Courts," *New York Times*, 16 February 1987, 1.

30. Gary Hengstler, "Scalia Seeks Court Changes," *American Bar Association Journal* 73 (1 April 1987), 20.

31. Taylor, 1.

32. Ibid., 12.

33. Hengstler, 20.

34. Taylor, 12.

35. Hengstler, 20.

36. Testimony of the Hon. Edward S. Northrup, Senate Committee on the Judiciary, *Federal Magistrates Act: Hearings Before the Subcommittee on Improvements in Judicial Machinery on S. 3475 and S. 945*, 89th Cong., 2d Sess, and 90th Cong., 1st Sess. (1966 and 1967), 52.

37. David Shapiro, "Federal Habeas Corpus: A Study in Massachusetts," *Harvard Law Review* 87 (1973): 366.

38. Christopher E. Smith, "Examining the Boundaries of *Bounds*: Prison Law Libraries and Access to the Courts," *Howard Law Journal* 30 (1987): 34–36.

39. Christopher E. Smith, "United States Magistrates and the Processing of Prisoner Litigation," *Federal Probation* 52 (December 1988): 15.

40. Christopher E. Smith, "From U.S. Magistrates to U.S. Magistrate Judges: Developments Affecting the Federal District Courts' Lower Tier of Judicial Officers," *Judicature* 75 (1992): 214, citing Bureau of Justice Statistics, "Prisoners in 1990," *Bureau of Justice Statistics Bulletin*, May 1991, 1.

41. "Statistics Reflect Active Year for Judiciary," *Third Branch* 26 (February 1994): 4–5.

42. Christopher E. Smith, "Judicial Lobbying and Court Reform: U.S. Magistrate Judges and the Judicial Improvements Act of 1990," *University of Arkansas-Little Rock Law Review* 14 (1992): 190.

43. Hoffman, 188.

44. Ibid.

45. Smith, "Judicial Lobbying," 171.

46. David M. O'Brien, *Storm Center: The Supreme Court in American Politics*, 2d ed. (New York: W. W. Norton, 1990), 128.

47. Christopher E. Smith, *Politics in Constitutional Law: Cases and Questions* (Chicago: Nelson-Hall, 1992), 94.

48. Linda Greenhouse, "Judges Challenge Rehnquist Action on Death Penalty: An Extraordinary Move," *New York Times*, 6 October 1989, A1, B7.

49. Rehnquist, 3; Yackle, 2361–2364.

50. Linda Greenhouse, "Scalia Tightens Policy on Death Penalty Appeals," *New York Times*, 22 February 1991, B16.

51. Teague v. Lane, 489 U.S. 288 (1989).

52. Penry v. Lynaugh, 492 U.S. 302 (1989).

53. Hoffmann, 166.

54. Ibid., 167.

55. J. Thomas Sullivan, "A Practical Guide to Recent Developments in Federal Habeas Corpus for Practicing Attorneys," *Arizona State Law Journal* 25 (1993): 317.

56. William H. Rehnquist, *This Honorable Court: Inside the Marble Temple* (documentary film broadcast 12 September 1989 on PBS).

57. See Christopher E. Smith and Avis Alexandria Jones, "The Rehnquist Court's Activism and the Risk of Injustice," *Connecticut Law Review* 26 (1993): 53–77.

58. Butler v. McKellar, 494 U.S. 407 (1990).

59. Arizona v. Roberson, 486 U.S. 675 (1988).

60. Butler v. McKellar, 494 U.S. at 414–416.

61. Butler v. McKellar, 494 U.S. at 431–432 (Brennan, J., dissenting).

62. See, e.g., Peter Irons, *The Courage of Their Convictions* (New York: Random House, 1988) (first-person narratives by people whose cases produced significant civil liberties decisions by the United States Supreme Court); Ellen Alderman and Caroline Kennedy, *In Our Defense: The Bill of Rights in Action* (New York: William Morrow, 1991) (illustrative accounts of individuals whose cases led to Supreme Court cases concerning the Bill of Rights).

63. Ruth Marcus, "Waiting Forever on Death Row," *Washington Post National Weekly Edition*, 18–24 June 1990, 11.

64. Christopher E. Smith, *Courts and the Poor* (Chicago: Nelson-Hall, 1991), 30.

65. Marcus, 11–12.

66. Ibid.

67. Ibid.

68. McCleskey v. Kemp, 481 U.S. 279 (1987).

69. Christopher E. Smith, "The Supreme Court and Ethnicity," *Oregon Law Review* 69 (1990): 829–830.

70. McCleskey v. Kemp, 481 U.S. at 287.

71. McCleskey v. Zant, 111 S. Ct. 1454 (1991).

72. Ibid., 1459–1460.

73. *Massiah v. United States*, 377 U.S. 201 (1964), was a groundbreaking Warren Court decision that forbade law enforcement officials to use informers to question a defendant outside of the presence of the defendant's attorney.

74. McCleskey v. Zant, 111 S. Ct. at 1474.

75. Savage, 414.

76. McCleskey v. Zant, 111 S. Ct. at 1458.

77. McCleskey v. Zant, 111 S. Ct. at 1489 (Marshall, J., dissenting).

78. Coleman v. Thompson, 111 S. Ct. 2546, 2552–2553. (1991).

79. Ibid., 2553.

80. Savage, 414.

81. Coleman v. Thompson, 111 S. Ct. at 2554–2555.

82. See Murray v. Giarratano, 492 U.S. 1 (1989) (no right to counsel for preparation of post conviction petitions by death-row inmates); Pennsylvania v. Finley, 481 U.S. 551 (1987) (no right to counsel in postconviction proceedings); Bounds v. Smith, 430 U.S. 817 (right of access to courts for prisoners satisfied by access to prison law library so prisoners can prepare their own petitions).

83. See, e.g., Abraham S. Blumberg, "The Practice of Law as a Confidence Game: Organization Co-optation of a Profession," *Law and Society Review* 1 (1967): 15 (analysis of how criminal defense attorneys' self-interest diminished forceful representation of clients' interests).

84. See William J. Bowers, "The Pervasiveness of Arbitrariness and Discrimination Under Post-Furman Capital Statutes," *Journal of Criminal Law and Criminology* 74 (1983): 37.

85. Coleman v. Thompson, 111 S. Ct. at 2569 (Blackmun, J., dissenting).

86. Ibid.

87. Jill Smolowe, "Must This Man Die?" *Time*, 18 May 1992, 43.

88. Ibid., 42.

89. Ibid.

90. Ibid., 42–43.

91. Ibid., 43.

92. Ibid., 44.

93. Smith and Jones, 75.

94. O'Dell v. Thompson, 112 S. Ct. 618 (1991) discussed in Linda Greenhouse, "Court Denial of Appeal Prompts Unusual Action," *New York Times*, 3 December 1991, B10.

95. Ibid.

96. Herrera v. Collins, 113 S. Ct. 853 (1993).

97. Ibid., 874–875 (Scalia, J., concurring).

98. Ibid., 875.

99. Ibid.

100. Ibid. ("With any luck, we shall avoid ever having to face this embarrassing question again, since it is improbable that evidence of innocence as convincing as today's opinion requires would fail to produce an executive pardon.").

101. Christopher E. Smith, "Habeas Corpus Reform: The View from the Federal District Courts" (Paper presented at the Midwestern Criminal Justice Association, Chicago, Illinois, 1994).

102. Ibid.

103. Ibid.

104. Ibid.

105. Ibid.

106. Ibid.

107. Jim Thomas, "The 'Reality' of Prisoner Litigation: Repackaging the Data," *New England Journal on Criminal and Civil Confinement* 15 (1989): 27–53.

108. See Shapiro, 1973; Richard Faust, Tina J. Rubenstein, and Larry W. Yackle, "The Great Writ in Action: Empirical Light on the Federal Habeas Corpus Debate," *New York University Review of Law and Social Change* 18 (1990–1991): 637–710.

109. "Crime Bill Moves Through House," *Third Branch* 26 (May 1994): 1–3.

110. Smith, *Courts, Politics, and the Judicial Process*, 12.

5

Systemic Developments: Judicial Bureaucracy

As federal judges sought assistance for dealing with their increasing caseload burdens, they supported the proliferation of judicial subordinates who could perform case-processing tasks under the ostensible supervision and control of judges. The creation of the U.S. magistrate judges, as discussed in previous chapters, was one example of a reform that increased the number and kinds of subordinates working for federal judges.

There is no reason to believe that judges have sought as a goal to increase the number of court personnel that they must supervise. Such personnel increase the administrative burdens on judges and draw them away from the activities that many of them prefer to spend their time undertaking— namely, judging. However, because judges cannot control legislative activities and can, in many instances, merely shape the court-related legislation that happens to reach the top of the legislative agenda, they have been forced to seek whatever resources the legislature has been willing to make available. Although some judges might prefer to see an increase in the number of judges, proposals for the creation of new judgeships can be the source of partisan conflict and stalemate within Congress. For example, when the Democrats control Congress, they are usually reluctant to create judgeships that will be filled by Republican presidential appointees. As a result, these judges may feel forced to support the proliferation of subordinate judicial personnel as the only available means to increase the judiciary's resources. Other judges have argued that there are too many federal judges already. Many of these judges would prefer to see a reduction in the number of cases permitted to enter the court system. If these judges are unable to persuade Congress to act or find other means to limit the numbers of cases filed in the federal courts, then they, too, may support additional judicial subordinates as the means to fulfill the judiciary's mission.

Thus the growth in judicial personnel is not a matter of simple self-interested preferences on the part of judges. However, the need for new resources that has forced judges to encourage the expansion of judicial personnel has challenged the judges' capacity to recognize and address the problems that may be attendant to the expansion of subordinates involved in decision making. Judges have a strong self-interest in maintaining the judiciary's image as a branch of government that functions smoothly and correctly, and this self-interest may lead them to deny or minimize the risks of detrimental effects that stem from the proliferation of subordinates.

Because of the increase in judicial personnel, warnings emerged from both judges and scholars during the 1970s about the "bureaucratization" of the courts.[1] Critics claimed that changes in courts' organizational structures and procedures adversely affected the proper performance of judicial institutions. It was asserted that only by responding quickly to these "alarm[s]" could American society "preserve [its] precious and imperilled courts as effective institutions."[2] Although Congress could act to restructure the courts and limit the numbers of judicial subordinates, it is far easier to create new positions than to reduce the numbers of staff members whom the judges have come to rely upon. Because judges oversee the activities of judicial subordinates, they bear the practical burden and responsibility for monitoring and remedying problems that may arise from "bureaucratization." The recognition and redress of such problems demands a level of introspection that may challenge individual judges' interests in and capacities for both self-criticism and the rearrangement of judicial responsibilities to place greater burdens upon themselves.

THE DEFINITION AND CONSEQUENCES OF "BUREAUCRACY"

In its most neutral sense, the term "bureaucracy" simply refers to the executive branch of government in its entirety or to individual agencies that comprise the executive branch. Although "bureaucracy" generally refers to the executive branch, the growth of internal and auxiliary agencies in the other branches of government has led observers to describe the legislative and judicial branches as "bureaucracies." Congress is characterized as a "legislative bureaucracy" because it employs more than 30,000 staff members and contains such agencies as the Congressional Budget Office, Office of Technology Assessment, and General Accounting Office.[3] Similarly, a central "judicial bureaucracy" developed in conjunction with the twentieth-century federal court system through the growth of the Administrative Office of the U.S. Courts (AO) and the Federal Judicial Center (FJC), which distribute resources, evaluate programs, and otherwise assist in the administration of the judicial system. The AO handles administrative tasks for the judicial branch, from assessing individual judges' requests for additional office equipment and staff to maintaining statistics on judicial officers' productivity to coordinating the judiciary's budget requests to Congress. The FJC provides training programs for new judges and other judicial officials, and it conducts research on the effectiveness of judicial programs and procedures.[4]

If the existence of "bureaucracy" merely indicated that organized agencies handle administrative responsibilities for the branches of government, people would pay scant attention to such a benign concept. The term "bureaucracy," however, conjures up powerful images for Americans. It has strong pejorative connotations of "incompetent, indifferent, bloated, and malevolent administrative departments of government."[5] Citizens who seek assistance from government agencies may feel that they have entered an impenetrable maze when they must shuffle from office to office, fill out dozens of official forms and documents, and endure interminable delays without ever identifying which faceless official possesses the decision-making power to ensure that the government provides the requested assistance. At its worst, the term "bureaucracy" implies a "concentration of power in administrative officials, excessive red tape, dedication to routine, and resistance to change."[6] The negative aspects of bureaucracy are not limited to the executive branch. Bureaucratic attributes can adversely affect the expected behavior of officials in other branches. In Congress, for example, senators and representatives increasingly spend their time supervising staff members and therefore have less time to debate issues and make policy decisions with their colleagues. By delegating responsibilities to their staffs, members of Congress inevitably place important decision-making power in the hands of unelected officials who are neither visible nor directly accountable to the voting public.

In the federal judiciary, the "bureaucratization problem" concerns developments affecting judicial officers within individual courthouses rather than the growth of centralized administrative agencies such as the AO and FJC. The federal courts have faced sharp increases in case filings. For example, although only 87,321 civil cases were filed in U.S. district courts in 1970, annual filings exceeded 200,000 cases during the late 1980s.[7] In addition, Congress passed many statutes that gave the federal courts authority over new issues and thereby encouraged more claimants to bring their cases to the federal judiciary. For example, anti-discrimination statutes that provide new protections for women and individuals with disabilities create opportunities to initiate additional cases in the federal court system. Because the federal courts became very active in defining and protecting the constitutional rights of individuals during the 1950s and 1960s, interest groups and individuals increasingly viewed the federal courts as appropriate forums for pursuing public policy initiatives that the executive and legislative branches were unwilling or unable to approve and implement. In response to these increased demands upon judicial resources, the judiciary and Congress introduced new procedures and added personnel to assist federal judges in their case-processing responsibilities.

In the federal courts, the foregoing developments have affected all three primary levels within the hierarchy of the court system, the trial courts (U.S. district courts), the intermediate appellate courts (U.S. circuit courts of appeals), and the court of last resort (United States Supreme Court). Because federal judges are the officials responsible for assigning and supervising tasks within federal courthouses, they must oversee and coordinate the activities of judicial subordinates. Although each level of the judicial branch has been affected in different ways, they have all arguably experienced adverse consequences from bureaucratization.

For the judiciary, the negative characteristics associated with bureaucratization, especially the delegation of tasks to subordinates and the supervision of growing courthouse staffs, create an environment that can be detrimental to the judicial process. In fact, bureaucratization arguably creates courts that are actually the antithesis of idealized judicial institutions. Ideally, learned judges apply their expertise in formulating carefully considered judgments about disputes that they have evaluated through first-hand examination of courtroom evidence and arguments. With bureaucratization, however, increasing caseload pressures and burgeoning responsibilities for the delegation of tasks and supervision of staff may force judges to make quick decisions based on subordinates' written summaries of cases or to approve routinely recommended decisions by subordinates. Judges may lose their capacity to make considered judgments about each case. In essence, courts may function more like stereotypical executive branch agencies in which decisions are made by faceless subordinates rather than by the visible figures empowered by the constitutional system to make the governing branch's important decisions that affect citizens' lives.

Such bureaucratic processes may be especially harmful in the judicial branch because they may threaten the legitimacy of the judiciary. People respect and obey judicial decisions, in part, because they accept the judiciary's special competence for deciding difficult issues and they trust the careful, fair, deliberative processes that are characteristic of the judicial branch.[8] As Owen Fiss observes,

By signing his [or her] name to a judgment or opinion, the judge assures the parties that he [or she] has thoroughly participated in that [judicial decision-making] process and assumes individual responsibility for the decision. We accept the judicial power on these terms, yet bureaucratization raises the spectre that the judge's signature is but a sham and that the judge is exercising power without genuinely engaging in the dialogue from which his [or her] authority flows.[9]

Commentators use the term "bureaucratization" to refer to several different developments affecting the federal courts. As identified by Wolf Heydebrand and Carroll Seron, "[t]here are at least four separate ways in which the notions of bureaucracy and, less frequently, routine administration are used in discussions of the organizational aspects of courts."[10] First, the concept has been applied to the routinization of judicial decisions because of burdensome filings of simple, repetitive cases. The processing of such cases can lead to routine, administrative decision making instead of the individualized deliberative processes normally associated with judicial decisions. Second, bureaucratization is said to result from changes in the case-processing methods of the federal district judges that have led them to emphasize alternative dispute resolution, settlement negotiations, and other techniques. These changes arguably alter judges' ideal judicial role from that of adjudicator in traditional adversarial proceedings to that of mediator and administrator in scheduling and monitoring cases through a series of alternative proceedings. Third, courthouse organization and procedures have led to the delegation of responsibilities to subordinate judicial actors. This form of bureaucratization has arguably dispersed decision-making authority to less visible officials who do not necessarily have the experience and protected tenure possessed by the regular federal judges who are empowered by the Constitution to be the governing system's independent judicial decision makers. Fourth, some commentators discuss bureaucratization in the context of the changing relationships among the legislative, executive, and judicial branches as the judiciary increasingly involves itself in the development and implementation of controversial social policies.[11]

This chapter will focus on the first and third of the foregoing characterizations of bureaucratic problems in the judicial branch. These characterizations concern the effects of the continuing bureaucratization "crisis" on judges' control over judicial decision making and their capacity to make careful, considered judgments in cases. As described by Judge Harry Edwards,

[This] conception of the pathology of bureaucratization rests on the diffusion of responsibility and the ultimate "Rule by Nobody." . . . [N]o one individual assumes responsibility for institutional output . . . [T]o the extent that [judicial subordinates] participate in the decision-making process, judges can no longer be viewed as individually responsible for their decisions.[12]

UNITED STATES SUPREME COURT

The United States Supreme Court is the symbolic and practical pinnacle of the American judicial system. The highest court's decisions interpret the meaning of the Constitution; establish precedents to be obeyed by all lower courts, both state and federal; and determine public policies on a variety of controversial issues, including criminal defendants' rights and abortion. Like other American courts, in recent decades the Supreme Court has experienced increased caseload pressures. Although the Supreme Court, unlike the trial courts and intermediate appellate courts, possesses the authority to select which cases it will hear, it must sort through thousands of petitions to determine which cases are worthy of its time and attention.

The overwhelming majority of cases arrive at the Supreme Court through petitions for a writ of certiorari (cert), which is simply a particular legal action that requests the Supreme Court to call up a case from a lower court. From 1951 to 1955, an average of 1,372 petitions was filed at the Supreme Court each year.[13] Twenty years later, the average had increased to nearly 4,000 petitions per year, and from 1986 to 1990, the average number of annual filings nearly reached 5,000.[14] The Court must screen these cases in order to select a small number for complete hearing and decision. During the 1992 Term, for example, the Court gave complete consideration to and issued decisions in fewer than 120 cases.[15]

As the number of cert petitions increased after the 1950s, the Supreme Court added personnel to assist the justices in screening and selecting cases for review. In particular, justices employed additional law clerks, recent graduates from the top law schools who spend one or two years working for one justice, normally after having spent one year working for a judge on a federal court of appeals. In the early 1950s, most justices employed two law clerks. By the 1980s, however, most justices employed four law clerks.[16] The law clerks bear primary responsibility for reviewing and summarizing certiorari petitions and for making recommendations to the justices concerning which cases should be accepted for hearing. The law clerks also conduct legal research and assist in drafting judicial opinions for their supervising justices in the cases that have been argued before the Court. For the justices on the Supreme Court, the increased caseload pressures and attendant growth in staff provide the conditions for two corresponding risks of judicial bureaucratization: quick, routine, and thereby potentially nonjudicious decisions about which cases to accept for hearing and undue decision-making influence by staff members who, because of their numbers, can no longer be closely supervised by judicial officers.

Justices' law clerks are relatively inexperienced lawyers, having usually spent only a single year out of law school as a clerk for a federal appellate judge prior to arriving at the Supreme Court. Despite their inexperience, however, the law clerks bear significant responsibility for evaluating certiorari petitions and assisting the justices in deciding which cases are sufficiently important to deserve the Court's attention. According to H. W. Perry, Jr., the "crucial" role played by law clerks in the case selection process has been understated in many scholars' analyses of Supreme Court decision making.[17] By sifting through the thousands of petitions, the law clerks play a role in determining which individual litigants will receive the Court's consideration and, in policy terms, in setting the Court's agenda for which public policy issues will receive judicial attention and influence. Because of the volume of petitions, there are significant risks that the law clerks cannot be adequately supervised by justices who are naturally preoccupied with studying lawyers' briefs and preparing opinions in cases that have already been accepted for argument. Thus the case selection process creates the greatest risks for the invasion of bureaucratic decision making within the Supreme Court because of the opportunity for law clerks to apply their own values in evaluating, summarizing, and characterizing the petitions that the justices must rely on in accepting cases.

In evaluating each certiorari petition, law clerks generally write a "cert memo," in which they summarize the petition and make recommendations to the justices about whether or not the case is worthy of acceptance. The justices make their decisions about which cases to accept based on the law clerks' cert memos. The justices always have the option of reading any petitions themselves if they so desire, but they usually do not have the time or the inclination to read the actual petitions. As the justices examine the cert memos in their chambers, the chief justice draws up a "discuss list" containing the cases that he deems sufficiently important to deserve discussion and consideration for inclusion among the accepted cases. Other justices can have cases added to the "discuss list" if they wish to have their colleagues consider accepting the cases for hearing. Relatively few cases are placed on the discuss list. According to David O'Brien, "[o]ver four-fifths of . . . cases are screened out by law clerks and never collectively discussed and considered by the justices."[18] At their regular weekly conferences, the justices vote on each case contained on the discuss list to decide whether or not it will be accepted. It requires the votes of four justices for a case to be accepted for full hearing.

If a case is not accepted for consideration, either because no justice asks for its inclusion on the discuss list or because fewer than four justices believe it is worthy of a complete decision, the effect is to preserve whatever decision was previously made in the case, usually either by a federal appeals court or by a state supreme court. A denial of certiorari does not constitute an endorsement by the Supreme Court of the lower court decision, but for the individual petitioner, it effectively keeps in place an adverse decision and signals that no favorable judicial action will be forthcoming. Some litigants may develop new evidence or a new legal theory upon which to base a future petition in the same case. The subsequent petition must work its way through the court system and may perhaps reach the Supreme Court again. Most cases end, however, when the Supreme Court decides not to hear them, and, therefore, the decision-making processes underlying the selection of cases have great importance for determining case outcomes for the 97 percent of cases filed with the Supreme Court that are never granted a hearing.

Originally, one law clerk for each justice wrote a cert memo for his or her supervising justice. Thus nine different law clerks read each petition, and this reduced the likelihood that the justices' selection decision would be adversely affected by missing information or biased characterizations of a petition's contents. If one justice's law clerk misinterpreted or mischaracterized some aspect of a petitioner's arguments through either inadvertence or bias, other justices would have more complete information available from their clerks' memos. In 1972, however, a majority of justices created a "cert pool," in which petitions were divided among the justices' chambers, so that a single law clerk wrote a cert memo concerning each petition and that memo was circulated among all of the justices participating in the pool.[19] Several justices remained outside of the pool, and, until his retirement in 1990, Justice William Brennan continued to look at most of the certiorari petitions himself. Since the formation of the cert pool, all of the new appointees have joined the pool, so that by 1992 only Justice John Paul Stevens had his own clerks write cert memos for him and his clerks write memos only in those cases that they deem to be important.[20]

The cert pool obviously saves time for the law clerks because, rather than examining 5,000 petitions annually in each justice's chamber, each participating justice's law clerks now handle only one-eighth of the Court's petitions. However, the cert pool also exacerbates the risk that petitions will not receive adequate consideration because now only one clerk generally reads each petition and the eight justices in the pool may rely on a single memo summarizing and characterizing a case in deciding whether to grant a hearing. If only one person examines a petition and justices rely on a cert memo from that person, there may be a greater risk that no one will counterbalance a subtly mischaracterized, biased, or otherwise incomplete summary of a case. Justices have a difficult enough time supervising their own four clerks in the process of drafting opinions. Can they adequately assess the quality of cert memos written by a single unfamiliar law clerk from some other justice's chambers?

Additional factors may detract from the ideal of careful consideration for each petition. First, because the petitions arrive at the Supreme Court throughout the year, the law clerks are frequently preoccupied with the more interesting tasks of drafting opinions and preparing memos concerning the cases accepted for argument while they continuously evaluate certiorari petitions. This burden of other more pressing and more interesting responsibilities may detract from the attention devoted by the law clerks to the never-ending supply of relatively routine petitions, which are, for the most part, inevitably destined for denial.

Second, the contents of the petitions may be difficult to analyze accurately. A significant number of the petitions are presented *pro se*, meaning by the petitioners themselves without the assistance of attorneys. Most of these petitions are filed *in forma pauperis* by people who, because of their financial circumstances, seek a waiver of the $200 filing fee. In 1989, 58 percent of the 5,746 cases on the Supreme Court's docket came from paupers' petitions.[21] Most of these pro se petitioners are prisoners seeking to have the Supreme Court examine some aspect of their conviction or the conditions of their incarceration. Many of these petitions are handwritten and contain jargon-filled claims by uneducated people who cannot communicate effectively in written English and, moreover, who lack the legal expertise necessary to effectively identify and present constitutional claims that deserve judicial attention.[22]

Although paupers' petitions have provided the basis for important Supreme Court decisions, the most famous being the decision establishing a right to counsel for indigent felony defendants,[23] these petitions are accepted for hearing at much lower rates than the cases presented by fee-paying petitioners. For example, one study showed that in 1978 the Court granted review to only 0.2 percent of paupers' petitions while the comparable percentage for paid cases was 7.8 percent.[24] This disparity may reflect the relative lack of legal merit in petitions presented by lay petitioners. However, it may also indicate the existence of bias among the influential decision makers (justices and law clerks), or it may provide evidence of the inadequacy of review by the inexperienced law clerks struggling with difficult-to-understand petitions. Chief Justice Earl Warren reportedly instructed his law clerks to compensate for the weaknesses in paupers' petitions by not only summarizing the points raised in the petition, but also raising any other point and making any other argument that the petitioner could have presented.[25] The practice of providing this extra attention to paupers' petitions apparently ended when Warren Burger succeeded Earl Warren as chief justice.[26]

The notion that law clerks may unduly influence Supreme Court decisions concerning the selection of cases for hearing was raised in the 1950s by future chief justice and then practicing attorney William Rehnquist. In two brief articles in a national news magazine, Rehnquist drew from his experience as a law clerk for Justice Robert Jackson in the early 1950s to assert that "from what I knew, the clerks taken as a whole were left of center, and that it was possible that their political views could to some extent influence the action of the Court in deciding whether to grant a hearing in a particular case."[27] When he later was appointed to the Supreme Court, Justice Rehnquist minimized the influence of law clerks on the Court's decisions. Like other judicial officers,[28] he is willing to raise concerns about external factors (e.g., rising caseloads) that hamper the effectiveness of courts and about the possibility that supervision may suffer if there are too many judicial personnel.[29] However, he (like other judges) is loathe to admit that internal decision-making processes have actually been adversely affected by bureaucratizing trends. According to Chief Justice Rehnquist, the justices have remained in touch with and in command of the case selection process:

Recently I was asked whether or not the use of the law clerks in a cert pool didn't represent the abandonment of the justices' responsibilities to a sort of internal bureaucracy. I certainly do not think so. . . . [T]he decision as to whether to grant certiorari is a much more "channeled" decision than the decision as to how a case should be decided on the merits; there are really only two or three factors comprised in the certiorari decision—conflict with other courts, general importance, and perception that the decision is wrong in light of Supreme Court precedent. Each of these factors is one that a well-trained law clerk is capable of evaluating, and the justices, of course, having been in the certiorari-granting business term after term, are quite familiar with many of the issues that come up.[30]

Although Chief Justice Rehnquist asserts that "a well-trained law clerk" will recognize the elements that lead justices to accept a case for hearing, questions remain about how the law clerks are trained. His description of his own training as a Supreme Court law clerk indicates that "training" consisted of "learning by doing" while asking questions of more senior clerks.[31] "Training" for contemporary clerks appears to have changed very little. While the justices are away during the summer break, they "train" their new law clerks by having the newcomers write cert memos with the advice of senior law clerks. According to Perry, "[t]here is little done in the way of teaching clerks what their justices want in a cert. memo. Clerks are expected to plunge into the cert. process and essentially learn on their own."[32] As described by O'Brien, this creates problems for the justices who must rely on the neophyte law clerks' memos in making case selection decisions at the beginning of the Supreme Court's annual term each October:

The problems of relying too much on clerks is apparent at the beginning of each term. . . . The justices now initiate their clerks, who come aboard in July, by having them write memos on the filings that arrive in the summer. The justices review these memos before their conference at the beginning of the term. Yet these memos are written by clerks who have little experience with the Court's rules and norms.[33]

Just as few people would want to be any lawyer's first client, the risk of error by inexperienced law clerks would lead petitioners, if they had any choice in the matter, to prefer evaluation by an experienced justice or at least by an experienced law clerk. Because of the workload created by the thousands of certiorari petitions, the justices have few alternatives to training law clerks by simply having them begin work. "Learning by doing" is obviously a more diplomatic way of saying "learning by trial and error" and this process, especially when employed in conjunction with the cert pool, increases the likelihood that at least some petitions will not receive careful consideration and proper evaluation by the inexperienced law clerks.

Even experienced law clerks who have evaluated certiorari petitions for several months can apply their personal values to judgments about the worthiness of cases. Social science studies of judicial decision making have provided ample evidence of the effects of judges' attitudes, background characteristics, experiences, and role orientations on court decisions.[34] Because law clerks are also intelligent, opinionated human beings, there is every reason to expect that they, too, inevitably insert their values into at least some decisions, even when they are trying to summarize petitions in accordance with the values of their supervising justice. As D. Marie Provine observed, "Although intended simply to summarize relevant legal issues for the justices' review decisions, the memos inevitably reflect the backgrounds of the law clerks who prepare them."[35] A study of certiorari memoranda by Chief Justice Fred Vinson's law clerks found that although the clerks generally tried to anticipate the chief justice's preferences with their recommendations, they evinced a liberal orientation in their case selection recommendations, and Chief Justice Vinson generally followed their suggestions.[36] This finding certainly raises the possibility that because the clerks' values and policy preferences are at least subtly embodied in their memoranda, the clerks may influence the justices' decisions concerning some cases.

Although independent influence by law clerks is moderated by any skepticism that justices may have about their clerks' recommendations and by the clerks' desire to please the justices by applying the justices' stated criteria,[37] there is still a risk of undue influence. Chief Justice Rehnquist himself inadvertently pointed to the likelihood of law clerks applying their own values when he described the "general importance of the case" as a primary criterion for selecting cases for hearing.[38] Assessments of "importance" require evaluative judgments that draw from personal attitudes and policy preferences. In most cases, justices may have their own definite ideas about whether or not a petition raises an "important" legal issue. In marginal cases, however—namely, those that are neither clearly important nor clearly unimportant—law clerks are likely to play key roles in identifying or failing to identify the potential importance of a case.

The risk of errors of omission may be greatest when a new law clerk, as the sole person from the cert pool who reads a particular petition, is responsible for evaluating a complicated and poorly written pauper's petition. Notwithstanding justices' confident and consistent assertions that they are in command of the case selection process, the high caseload of petitions, including difficult-to-evaluate paupers' petitions, and the formation of the cert pool have created an environment in which relatively inexperienced law clerks can influence an important stage in the Court's decision-making process and thereby effectively determine outcomes in some cases.

Law clerks can also influence the opinions issued by the Court. Justice Stevens clearly illustrated this point in a documentary film concerning the Supreme Court:

Justice Stevens: [pointing to law clerk]: "One [case] that you convinced me to change my mind on, you remember? You convinced me once, but then I think I got unconvinced."

Law Clerk: "Then you got reconvinced again."

Justice Stevens: "Reconvinced. . . . We went back and forth on it several times."[39]

A study of law clerks in state supreme courts and federal appellate courts found that they undertook extra work and prepared additional information when they felt strongly enough about an issue to attempt to persuade their supervising justice or judge about the appropriate outcome.[40] This kind of influence is consistent with a primary function of the first law clerks early in the twentieth century. According to the famous jurist Judge Learned Hand, the law clerk's primary function was "to serve as a wall against whom the judge bounced balls."[41] By drawing from the ideas and feedback provided by bright subordinates, judicial officers can better develop and refine their own opinions.

However, larger numbers of law clerks may alter the opinion-development process at the Supreme Court by focusing a justice's deliberative interactions on subordinates rather than on colleagues.[42] Instead of actively discussing cases with other justices, the justices may be more involved with bouncing ideas off of their own clerks and rewriting their clerks' draft opinions. It is difficult to surmise whether or not this represents a detrimental development that deserves to be characterized as a bureaucratization "problem." A reduction in personal interaction may affect collegiality among the justices, but collegiality is also very much a function of the individual personalities and work styles of the individuals who serve as justices at any given moment in history. Moreover, the final work product—namely, the Court's opinions—may not be significantly different whether or not the justices speak with each other in person or merely circulate draft opinions.

In addition, some justices' law clerks have played a primary role in determining what a justice's opinion will say. During the 1940s, for example, Justice Frank Murphy gained a reputation for permitting his clerks to actually write his opinions for him.[43] This differs from the usual practice of having clerks write rough drafts that are subsequently rewritten and refined by the justices themselves.[44]

INTERMEDIATE APPELLATE COURTS

Intermediate appellate courts have been called "the workhorses of the appellate court process."[45] Unlike courts of last resort, which usually have significant discretionary jurisdiction and therefore can select which cases they deem sufficiently important to hear and decide, intermediate appellate courts generally have mandatory jurisdiction over most appeals. They must decide the cases presented to them. Because of caseload pressures, however, they cannot hear every case that they must decide. Thus intermediate appellate courts frequently decide cases in a summary fashion based on the written submissions from appellants, and, increasingly, the courts do not publish explanatory judicial opinions in cases that they decide.

Intermediate appellate courts have experienced significant increases in their caseloads. The number of appeals filed in federal courts of appeals increased from 27,946 in 1982 to 40,898 in 1990.[46] The caseload burdens experienced by intermediate appellate courts have led to a proliferation of staff to assist in the processing of cases. According to Judge Alvin Rubin, the growth in staff has an "adverse impact" because "as [appellate] judges become busier, they have less time to communicate with each other. . . . [in order] to harmonize opinions and reach collegial decisions."[47]

Appellate judges have law clerks to assist them with conducting legal research and drafting opinions, although they generally have fewer clerks (one or two) than the justices on the United States Supreme Court, who generally have four clerks. The law clerks write memoranda summarizing cases that judges rely on when preparing to hear oral argument. The clerks also assist in drafting opinions and orders for both cases that are heard in oral argument and cases that receive summary decisions based on written submissions. Unlike in the United States Supreme Court, where the exercise of discretionary jurisdiction limits the number of cases accepted for hearing and thereby provides greater opportunities for justices to read the litigants' briefs prior to hearing oral arguments, in intermediate appellate courts judges are more likely to be dependent on summaries written by their subordinates. As indicated by J. Woodford Howard's study of federal appellate courts,

> Prior to oral argument most judges seldom do more than scan pertinent portions of the record called to their attention by clerks or counsel. . . . To prepare for oral argument, all but a handful of circuit judges rely upon bench memoranda prepared by their law clerks, plus their own notes from reading briefs. . . . For their perceptions of issues prior to decision, circuit judges are increasingly dependent upon the homework of others.[48]

This reliance creates risks that judges' understanding of cases and subsequent decisions in those cases are shaped by experienced subordinates' analysis of written arguments. Although judges have opportunities to learn more for themselves during oral arguments (for those cases that are selected for oral presentation), the effectiveness of oral argument is diminished by its brevity (often only one hour), the variable quality of appellate advocacy presented by attorneys who gain little training in such skills during law school, and the confusing press of multiple unrelated cases that are argued one after another. Judges necessarily rely on law clerks in preparing to decide cases, but that reliance may detract from the judicial ideal of considered judgments by experienced, informed judges when an appellate court is grappling with a significant caseload.

Staff attorneys constitute a second important category of personnel who assist judges with decision making in intermediate appellate courts. Staff attorneys in the federal circuit courts and the appellate courts of many states frequently screen filings to assist judges in deciding which cases deserve oral arguments and complete judicial decisions.[49] Staff attorneys also write the courts' opinions in many cases that are decided in a summary fashion.

Appellate judges have the opportunity to supervise law clerks closely because the judges usually have only one or two clerks and the clerks work very hard to please their supervising judges. This does not eliminate the possibility of improper influence by law clerks over case outcomes, but it diminishes the potential for the worst-case scenario of bureaucratic decision making beyond the knowledge and control of the authoritative judicial officers.

By contrast, the staff attorneys employed by intermediate appellate courts create significant risks that unknown decision makers are determining judicial outcomes without direct supervision from judges. Unlike law clerks, staff attorneys possess a degree of independence that raises serious questions about the bureaucratization of appellate decisions beyond the control of judicial officers. They are not selected by and loyal to any particular judge. According to Judge Richard Posner, the potential problems with staff attorneys extend beyond their loyalty to the indistinct entity of a court rather than to an individual judge:

There can be no assurance that the staff attorney will share the outlook and values of the judge, and he will not have a chance to acquire that outlook and those values . . . by working continuously with the same judge for a substantial period of time [as a law clerk does].[50]

In addition, because staff attorneys are permanent employees, rather than one- or two-year employees like judges' law clerks, they resemble the permanent law clerks used in some state courts, who, according to the most well known study of law clerks, create "risks of either the devolution of judicial power upon nonjudicial officers or the evolution of stimulating law clerks into bureaucrats."[51]

Howard's study of the federal circuit courts demonstrated that many judges are sensitive to concerns that decision making will take on bureaucratic characteristics. Several, but not all, federal appellate courts have adopted procedures to reduce the risk that judges will lose control over decision making.[52] At the time of Howard's study (the 1970s), for example, in the Eighth Circuit cases were screened by the judges, presumably with the assistance of law clerks, rather than by staff attorneys. The Fourth Circuit required written opinions when oral arguments were denied, and the Tenth Circuit eliminated staff recommendations on case outcomes in order to avoid excessive delegation.[53] In the Fifth Circuit, however, which Howard studied before it was divided into two circuits (the Fifth and Eleventh Circuits), the attributes of bureaucratization were evident. Judges admitted that they lacked the time to read the litigants' briefs until after staff attorneys had already written decisions on behalf of the court.[54] Without the judges taking a fresh, open-minded look at the respective sides' arguments before reading a decision favoring one side, there is a great risk that the judges will simply endorse or, in its most pejorative characterization, "rubber-stamp," the decisions of staff attorneys.

Because appellate decisions are made by three-judge panels and most decisions are unanimous, it might appear that group decision making safeguards against the possibility that any single judge might give inadequate consideration to a case. However, this apparent safeguard provides no guarantee of careful, considered judgments when, as in the Fifth Circuit, all three judges made their decision while relying on the very same bench memo from one staff attorney summarizing the case and recommending an outcome.[55]

In the Fifth Circuit, nearly all summary dispositions of cases considered not worthy of oral argument were decided " 'round-robin style,' by mail or phone" as the judges merely contacted each other and reached agreement.[56] In one-quarter of these cases, the parties were given no explanation whatsoever for the court's decision.[57] Such decisions raise especially grave risks that the judicial subordinates are determining the outcomes of cases. If judges reach decisions by relying on staff attorneys' (or law clerks') summaries and recommendations without discussing the cases with colleagues or without applying the systematic analysis required for drafting an opinion, the judges may be thoughtlessly "rubber-stamping" decisions made by staff members. The appellate processes of discussing cases with other judges on the appeals court and developing carefully written opinions serve as the primary means to ensure that the judges have engaged in thorough, deliberative processes. When those elements are missing, decision-making processes may become routine and manifest bureaucratic attributes.

In addition, the utilization of staff attorneys for screening processes "raised the spectre of unequal justice to underprivileged litigants."[58] While more than 70 percent of tax law cases and cases concerning federal law were granted oral arguments, more than 90 percent of cases from prisoners unrepresented by attorneys were given summary decisions. Similarly, other cases involving less affluent litigants, such as Social Security disability claims and criminal appeals, were usually disposed of through summary decisions. As Howard noted, "Efficiency experts might commend this as a rational allocation of judicial manpower, segregating for summary treatment routine appeals that would not benefit from oral argument. But who is to say what is junk litigation? Why were petitioners with counsel much more likely to be heard than those without?"[59]

Although Howard's famous study was conducted during the 1970s, his observations on the risks and problems of reliance on judicial staff continue to have validity because subsequent increases in caseload pressures have created an environment that requires the use of staff attorneys in the processing of cases in even more federal and state appellate courts. According to Judge Posner, the number of law clerks in federal district courts and the United States Supreme Court merely doubled between 1960 and the mid–1980s, but over the same time span the number of law clerks and staff attorneys in federal circuit courts quadrupled.[60] While Howard's study during the 1970s might have created the impression that bureaucratization problems were focused in the Fifth Circuit, a 1991 study indicated that ten of the twelve federal circuit courts of appeals relied heavily on staff attorneys to screen cases.[61]

Staff attorneys also play an increasingly important role in drafting published appellate court opinions and in actually authoring unpublished opinions that are issued under the names of judges. According to Judge Posner, "a significant number of published court of appeals opinions are drafted by a staff attorney rather than by a judge or one of his law clerks."[62] Because this opinion drafting is undertaken by someone who is not supervised by an individual judge and therefore has not become familiar with and has not learned to emulate the decision-making criteria of a particular judge, the staff attorneys must inevitably apply their own analysis and values. The judges have the opportunity to rewrite such drafts, but they may lack the time and inclination to monitor closely the reasoning presented in every case by staff attorneys, which will effectively become part of appellate court precedents.

Staff attorneys may have even more involvement in unpublished opinions because those are written in cases concerning issues that are considered insufficiently important to require dissemination of a court's reasoning. Because recent research has raised questions about whether cases decided with unpublished opinions can accurately be classified as concerning "unimportant" issues,[63] staff attorneys may be determining outcomes in cases that require difficult judgments and that inevitably require substantial application of a decision maker's values. The constitutional governing system vests duly appointed judges with the power to make such decisions, but staff attorneys lack the necessary visibility and authority to properly bear responsibility for determining case outcomes.

Although it came from a state court context, a 1992 study of the role of staff attorneys in Michigan's intermediate appellate court provided interesting insights on the possibility that staff attorneys determine case outcomes in appellate courts, including similarly structured federal courts. Not only did the study's findings raise important questions, but also the subsequent reactions of judicial officials who objected to the study's implications further illuminated the environment for bureaucratic decision making that exists in appellate courts. In their study, Mary Lou Stow and Harold Spaeth found very high levels of agreement between judges' decisions and preceding recommendations by staff attorneys, both short-term prehearing attorneys (serving two-year terms on the court's central staff) and permanent "commissioners."[64] The authors found the results "disturbing" because they had reason to discount the possibility that outcomes in cases appeared obviously "open and shut" to both staff attorneys and judges or that the staff attorneys had succeeded in internalizing the judges' decisional criteria and preferences.[65]

A judge from Michigan and staff attorneys from other states subsequently objected to the study's implication that staff attorneys make substantive decisions for appellate courts. However, the critics inadvertently highlighted the risks of bureaucratization by arguing that high caseloads make staff attorneys a necessity and that the outcomes in many cases are "obvious" and therefore high agreement rates between staff attorneys and judges should be expected.[66] As Stow and Spaeth noted, "If the judges, [in the words of one judge-critic] simply could not keep pace' without central staff, then it seems clear that the judges are relying very heavily on staff."[67] Moreover, if staff attorneys are merely making self-evident decisions in sorting the "wheat" from the "chaff" among the cases for the judges, "don't attorneys in appellate practice and citizens alike have a right to know? The facade of *judicial* rulings could be discontinued, and the wasted time and docket space avoided. Central staff could settle in as a chaff-processing bureaucracy, leaving wheat for real consideration by judges."[68] However, it is obvious that any forthright admission that cases are treated differently within the appellate process would fly in the face of public expectations about equal treatment for litigants and considered judgments from the judicial branch. Thus the defensive denials expressed by judicial officials are both predictable and understandable.

The proliferation and relative autonomy of staff attorneys have led commentators to attack sharply the risks that the staffers pose to careful judicial decision making by appellate judges. Former Solicitor General of the United States Wade McCree referred to the expansion of appellate staff attorneys as a "cancerous growth," and he claimed to "have seen many [appellate judicial] opinions in the last few years that contain substantial internal evidence of cursory judicial examination [of the staff attorneys' handiwork]."[69] According to McCree, "[i]t is not at all rare to see unpublished, per curiam opinions [i.e., on behalf of the court rather than from any single judge] containing obvious logical—and even grammatical—flaws, all carried beneath the names of three judges whose published opinions generally demonstrate clear thinking and precise writing."[70] Owen Fiss of Yale Law School advocates "abolishing the [staff attorney] position altogether. . . . [because of his] belief that staff attorneys pose too great a risk of diffusing responsibility, precisely because they are responsible to no particular judge."[71] According to Fiss, "[t]he use of staff attorneys to screen so-called 'meritless' cases not only produces an anonymous form of justice, but tends to insulate judges from the ebb and flow of the law and the full impact of grievances presented."[72]

By contrast, judicial officers' concerns, whether conscious or unconscious, about preserving the image and legitimacy of the judicial branch apparently hinder any admission that bureaucratic decision making actually occurs within the courts. Even Judge Posner, the insightful jurist-scholar, declines to admit that significant problems yet exist in judicial decision making. Judge Posner has documented the risks of reliance on law clerks and staff attorneys and has concluded that the federal courts are a " 'bureaucracy' in its popular sense of a large, unwieldy organization tenuously held together by paper."[73] Despite his conclusion that any further growth in law clerks and staff attorneys would be "counterproductive,"[74] he confidently declares that "[t]he process of delegation to law clerks (and staff attorneys) has not reached the point where decisional function itself has been delegated."[75]

These claims that judicial decision making has not been affected by bureaucratization raise many important questions. Can Posner or anyone else really make such an assertion regarding all federal judges in all federal courts? Federal judges vary in their capacities to evaluate the processes taking place in their courts and to take steps to assert control over decision making. Is the federal judiciary currently at the optimum level or, alternatively, at its maximum tolerance point for the employment of legal assistants, or has that point already been exceeded? Since Judge Posner says that the addition of any more staff members would be detrimental, can he really be certain that adverse consequences are not already occurring in light of the tremendous expansion in staff, especially in intermediate appellate courts? Does Judge Posner's conclusion take into account his own recognition of "the temptation to judicial carelessness that comes from having a staff of eager young assistants quite willing to take responsibility from the judge's shoulders"?[76] Similarly, Chief Justice Rehnquist says that "a federal judiciary rising above 1,000 members . . . could be dominated by a bureaucracy of ancillary personnel."[77] With a federal judiciary containing nearly 750 judges, why is this not already a problem? Judges are cognizant of the risks to judicial decision making posed by bureaucratization, but if their self-interest in preserving the judicial image makes them unwilling to admit that detrimental consequences have occurred, they diminish the incentives and opportunities for close examination of whether current decision-making processes actually fulfill proper judicial functions.

Individual judges, such as Judge Harry Edwards, have raised concerns about these issues. Thus the subtle pressures of judicial self-interest have not produced complete denial about the potential risks. However, because of the decentralized and fragmented nature of court organization, the recognition and redress of such problems required individual judges throughout the country to take a long, hard look at their own courthouses and chambers. The risk of bureaucratization looms largest when viewed in the aggregate context because of the clash between detrimental consequences for judicial decision making and judges' self-interested impulses toward denial.

FEDERAL TRIAL COURTS

The U.S. district courts have experienced the bureaucratizing impact of burgeoning case management responsibilities that arguably alter the judges' roles,[78] and they also have grappled with the growth of staff personnel who require supervision and management by the district judges. As described by Judge Rubin,

To meet his [or her] responsibilities, the federal district judge today has, in addition to a secretary and two law clerks, a docket clerk assigned by the clerk's office, a court reporter, the services of a probation staff and the assistance of a magistrate [judge] and the magistrate [judge's] staff. He hears appeals from matters handled by bankruptcy judges and reviews the work of the magistrate [judge]. In effect, he runs a small law firm.[79]

According to Judge Rubin, it is impossible for contemporary federal judges to supervise completely the work of subordinates: "However hard a judge tries, he [or she] cannot completely review everything that his [or her] law clerks do. . . . Inevitably they assist [the judge] not only in routine tasks but in the work of judging."[80]

One particularly important change in the federal trial courts has been the introduction of new personnel, most notably the U.S. magistrate judge.[81] Because the magistrate judges are subordinates to the district judges, yet vested with broad authority and provided with their own support staffs, the federal district courts embody an environment with particularly great risks for the bureaucratizing effects on judicial decision making that stem from growth in judicial personnel.

The creation of new federal judgeships involves significant partisan political considerations. Unless the White House and Congress are controlled by the same political party, opposition members of Congress are unlikely to support the creation of judgeships when a president from the opposing party will have the opportunity to fill those judgeships with partisan supporters. Thus, for example, despite escalating caseload pressures during the 1970s and 1980s, the only significant creation of new judgeships occurred during the Carter administration when Democrats controlled both Congress and the presidency.

During the 1960s, Congress sought to avoid such partisan problems that hindered the expansion of judicial resources by creating a new judicial office, the U.S. magistrate judge, that would be filled through appointments made by district judges for whom the new official would work rather than by the president. As discussed in prior chapters, although these subordinate judicial officers are visible to the public primarily only in their duties of handling criminal arraignments and setting bail, magistrates can actually supervise hearings for a variety of preliminary criminal and civil matters. They can even preside as authoritative judges over complete civil trials if both litigants voluntarily consent.[82] The importance of magistrate judges is evident in the number of matters that they take responsibility for in the district courts. In 1990, magistrate judges handled 450,565 matters, including 5,112 Social Security appeals, 20,583 prisoners' cases, and 1,008 complete civil trials.[83]

Magistrate judges' roles and responsibilities vary from district to district depending on such factors as district judges' attitudes about their subordinates' proper roles, caseload demands within particular districts, and the degree of communication between magistrate judges and district judges.[84] Congress granted broad authority to the magistrate judges, but it could not require that district judges utilize magistrate judges for the full breadth of that authority. Because of the desire for flexible utilization of this judicial resource and the reluctance to intrude on district judges' authority over case processing, Congress encouraged district courts to utilize magistrate judges broadly while it recognized that the subordinate judicial officers' actual roles would be determined by the needs of each district court. As a result, while magistrate judges in some districts perform almost as if they are district judges with their own civil trial caseload, magistrate judges in other districts are virtually permanent law clerks who perform limited tasks under close supervision of district judges.

Carroll Seron's study of magistrate judges' roles in federal district courts revealed that the subordinate judicial officers could be placed in three general categories.[85] In some districts, magistrate judges were "Additional Judges," who handled their own caseloads of civil litigation. In other districts, magistrate judges were "Team Players," who handled specific preliminary stages of civil and criminal cases, such as evidentiary hearings and settlement conferences, as they prepared the cases for eventual trials before district judges. Magistrate judges elsewhere were "Specialists," who devoted most of their time to limited categories of cases, primarily involving prisoners and Social Security disability claimants, in districts with heavy loads of these cases.[86]

Magistrate judges can make final determinations on dispositive matters—namely, rulings that dispose of the case—only when the litigants consent. When district judges assign magistrate judges to handle dispositive motions such as motions for summary judgment, unless the litigants consent to having the magistrate judge handle the case, the district judge must take a recommendation from the magistrate judge before issuing a ruling under the district judge's signature. For nondispositive matters, such as preliminary hearings to determine the admissibility of evidence, the magistrate judge may make the authoritative ruling.

Although these procedures are designed to ensure that district judges actually control judicial decision making, especially concerning matters that will determine the outcomes of cases, magistrate judges are actually very influential. Nondispositive motions decided by a magistrate judge may not terminate a case immediately, but such rulings may ultimately determine the case's outcome. If a magistrate judge rules that a certain piece of evidence is inadmissible, for example, the case may formally continue, but if the evidence was crucial to one side's case, this "nondispositive" ruling may actually have determined which party will prevail in subsequent settlement negotiations or at trial. Litigants may ask district judges to review magistrate judges' rulings on nondispositive matters, but the district judges apply a limited standard of review: "A district judge will review magistrate [judges'] findings on appeal according to the 'clearly erroneous' or 'contrary to law' standards, limited reviews which clearly vest magistrate [judges] with significant judicial decision-making authority because the [district] judges are not second-guessing the magistrate [judges'] judgments."[87] Thus magistrate judges may be important decision makers if district judges permit them to exercise their authority by assigning a variety of tasks to these judicial subordinates.

When magistrate judges assume the role of "Additional Judges" or "Team Players," they become important decision makers in the litigation process. Their exercise of decision-making authority raises questions about the propriety of delegating judicial authority to officials who do not fit the Constitution's definition of judges. Under Article III of the Constitution, federal judges are given the independence to make courageous, unpopular decisions because they serve "during good Behaviour," which effectively means for life, and their salaries cannot be reduced. In addition, these judges are selected by the president and confirmed by Senate, so there is an indirect democratic accountability mechanism: If the public does not like the decisions produced by the judiciary, the public can always vote for new presidents and senators who will appoint different kinds of lawyers to be judges. Because magistrate judges serve for eight-year renewable terms and they are appointed and reappointed by the district judges for whom they work, they do not fit the constitutional model for independent judicial decision makers who are connected to the electorate through appointment and confirmation by democratically elected officials.[88] Members of Congress who opposed the creation of this new judicial office analogized the impropriety of magistrate judges' decision-making authority to the unthinkable possibility of permitting elected representatives and senators to authorize their assistants to cast votes for them in Congress.[89] Magistrate judges' lack of independence may adversely affect their decisions, especially in an increasingly bureaucratized judicial branch.

There are risks that in seeking to keep their jobs magistrate judges may try so hard to please the district judges with their decisions that they may lack the independence to make comprehensive, open-minded evaluations of matters presented to them for decision. On the surface, it may appear to be unproblematic if magistrate judges attempt to shape their decisions in accordance with the district judges' values. After all, this process would appear to counteract bureaucratization by having the actual judges, rather than their subordinates, control decision making. In fact, however, such decision making can raise the specter of bureaucratic "rubber-stamping" of inadequately considered judgments. Magistrate judges may make decisions based on their *perception* of how a particular district judge would decide the case. The district judge may then approve the decision based on the *assumption* that the magistrate judge has decided the case in accordance with the district judge's values and methods. However, what if the magistrate judge's perception of the district judge's probable decision is wrong? There may never be an open-minded decision on the issue, and the district judge may approve the decision without ever examining it closely to see if it comports with his or her preferences.[90] This scenario represents a stereotypical "rubber-stamped" decision that is the antithesis of the considered judgments that are expected in judicial decision making.

The existence of authoritative judicial subordinates has also created documented instances of district judges pressuring litigants to waive their option of having civil cases heard by actual district judges. The availability of alternative decision makers within the district court's hierarchy permits self-interested judges to coerce litigants to consent to magistrate judges' authority by setting unreasonable deadlines for civil litigation and trials that will only be adjusted if the litigants accept transfer to a magistrate judge's supervision.[91] These events occurred despite congressional efforts to avoid such coercion by wording the magistrate judges' authorizing statute prior to 1990 to specifically prohibit district judges and magistrate judges from discussing the consent option with litigants. In some districts, judges did not comply with the statutory prohibition, and litigants consented to the magistrate judges' jurisdiction precisely because the litigants' "lawyers feel that they have little choice but to go along with the [district judge's] suggestion."[92] Such coercive tactics are not subtle when applied to litigants' attorneys, yet they remain virtually impossible to police: "[S]cheduling trial dates and refusing continuances are part of a judge's prerogatives. . . . [and] [t]hus the coercive actions [are] cloaked in the impenetrable discretionary authority of judges."[93]

The risk of such bureaucracy-generated pressures increased in 1990 when the statute was altered to permit district judges and magistrate judges to directly raise the consent trial option with litigants and their attorneys.[94] The statute was revised for the laudable and benign reason of encouraging more flexible use of judicial resources (i.e., permitting magistrate judges to provide maximum authorized assistance for district courts). However, district judges may use the revised statute to behave in a self-interested fashion in order to shed their responsibilities for cases that they consider boring, uninteresting, or annoying. Thus the well-intentioned statutory revision will effectively permit unconscientious district judges to exploit the existence of the district courts' bureaucratic hierarchy of decision-making professionals. Such actions will adversely affect litigants who are presumably entitled to have their cases decided by constitutionally empowered judges rather than by statutorily created judicial subordinates.

Magistrate judges who are utilized as "Specialists" in prisoner and Social Security cases are especially susceptible to slipping into bureaucratic decision making. Frequently, magistrate judges become "Specialists" because their district courts bear a significant burden of filings in these categories of cases, that are considered by district judges to be routine and uninteresting. Many magistrate judges also view these cases as burdensome and boring because they aspire to do more interesting tasks such as presiding over hearings and trials in the civil litigation process.[95] Thus the magistrate judges may attempt to dispense with these cases as quickly as possible in order to make themselves available for more interesting task assignments.

In Social Security cases, the magistrate judges review denials of disability benefits that were determined by administrative law judges (ALJs) in the Social Security Administration. The magistrate judge does not undertake a complete reconsideration of the ALJ's decision; he or she merely looks to see whether there is evidence to support the ALJ's decision to deny benefits. As a result, most cases are simple affirmances of the previous decision. Prisoners' cases are also seldom successful. Most are dismissed immediately and fewer than 4 percent proceed to any ultimate judicial decision on the merits.[96] Because prisoners are generally submitting their legal filings on their own without the assistance of counsel, they lack the training necessary to identify legitimate legal claims, and they lack the education and experience to make effective presentations of their arguments, even if they possess valid claims.

Because these two categories of claimants are so frequently unsuccessful, there are serious risks that magistrate judges begin with a presumption of dismissal, rather than an open-minded examination of these cases, especially when faced with a burdensome caseload. One study found that magistrate judges and their staffs began their examinations of prisoners' cases by asking "How can I dismiss this case?" rather than considering "Does this complaint contain any valid constitutional claims?"[97] For most cases, either initial question may result in a dismissal because so many prisoners' cases lack legal merit. However, in a case that contains a valid claim that has been poorly presented, the magistrate judge's initial posture may affect his or her ability to identify the meritorious "wheat" among the "chaff" of invalid claims.

In Social Security cases, magistrate judges should ideally review each claimant's medical records, which are frequently voluminous, in order to determine whether the medical evidence supports the ALJ's decision that the person is not entitled to disability benefits. Some magistrate judges, however, have been quite open about how they have routinized their review process, thus making their decisions according to bureaucratic rather than judicial methods:

One magistrate [judge] reportedly used a checklist to have law clerks quickly affirm ALJ decisions without thoroughly reading the records of each case. Other magistrate [judges] claimed that they could decide cases merely by seeing which lawyer represented the claimant. Another magistrate [judge] claimed that he could review dozens of [Social Security] cases at home in a single evening, an obvious indication that the large medical record file accompanying each case was not reviewed comprehensively. Yet another magistrate [judge] was quoted as saying, "Virtually all Social Security appeals are from people who should never qualify."[98]

Some magistrate judges regard Social Security cases as "more important than any corporate litigation involving millions of dollars, because . . . disabled people may need the few hundred dollars each month from Social Security in order to survive."[99] Presumably these magistrate judges make an effort to give these cases careful attention, despite the relatively routine and repetitive nature of such cases. Other magistrate judges, however, apparently treat these cases as less important than other cases and less worthy of complete review.[100]

The bureaucratic elements of decision making become exacerbated because the magistrate judges have their own support staffs separate from those of the district judges. Magistrate judges have their own law clerks to assist with research and opinion writing. They may also receive recommendations from *pro se* clerks, who, in some courts, work solely on reviewing and making recommendations concerning filings from individuals (i.e., primarily prisoners) who present claims without the assistance of attorneys. These *pro se* clerks are similar to appellate staff attorneys because they work for the trial court, rather than for any specific judicial officer, and therefore may lack direct supervision. In many cities with nearby law schools, magistrate judges as well as district judges employ law students as part-time interns who can assist with research and writing.[101] The existence of so many staff members with legal training, and therefore eligible for delegated duties in reviewing prisoner and Social Security cases, creates nightmarish risks of bureaucratic decision making within an extended hierarchy.

In many courthouses, a prisoner's petition or a Social Security disability appeal is assigned to a specific district judge. That judge may ask his or her law clerk whether the law clerk would like to handle the case because some district judges permit their law clerks to determine which tasks will be delegated to magistrate judges.[102] Because such cases are not considered interesting or important, the district judge's law clerk will probably refer the case to the magistrate judge. The magistrate judge then assigns the case to his or her law clerk. That law clerk may, in turn, delegate the case to the part-time law student intern because, with the high dismissal rates, those are precisely the kinds of cases that are regarded as requiring minimal analytical skill. Thus the individual at the bottom of the hierarchy, whether a law student or a magistrate judge's law clerk, reads the file and drafts a recommended decision, usually a dismissal or a denial of benefits. The recommendation is passed up the hierarchy and potentially gains automatic approval from each superior decision maker who is preoccupied with more interesting responsibilities. Ultimately, the district judge may sign off on a decision that was developed and authored by the only person to read the file; a person who also happens to be the least experienced and lowest status actor in the court's hierarchy. With so many layers of decision makers, there are risks that cases that are considered less interesting or less important will be inadequately considered by inexperienced decision makers and then "rubber-stamped" by superior judicial officers.

CONCLUSION

A natural response to increasing caseload pressures is to increase the resources available to assist in courts' case-processing responsibilities. Judges cannot readily control the legislative agenda either to produce limits on cases entering the court system or to initiate their ideal version of resource-enhancing legislation. Moreover, it can be expensive to create new judgeships because of the need to build new courtrooms and hire the staff necessary to support a judge. In addition, the prospect of creating new judgeships often generates maneuvering by competing political parties who wish to prevent their opponents from gaining any advantage in filling these authoritative positions with partisans. Thus political stalemates often block the passage of legislation necessary for the creation of new judgeships. As a result, Congress has found it easier and less expensive to expand the support staff for federal appellate and trial judges. Federal judges have generally supported the proliferation of judicial subordinates because of their perceived need for greater assistance with case-processing responsibilities and because the creation of judicial subordinates places control over new court resources and innovations directly within the judges' hands. The alternative approach, as described in Chapter 2, when Congress initiates new procedures designed to affect how judicial resources are employed, is most likely to produce effective legislation-shaping (or legislation-blocking) reactions by judges, and thus it is easier to simply add personnel.

The judges' self-interest in this case is both personal and institutional. The growing caseload burden requires the creation of politically acceptable and relatively inexpensive resources, such as judicial subordinates. At the same time, the proliferation of such subordinates eases the workload personally experienced by judges, especially with respect to less interesting and less desirable tasks. Moreover, the expansion of judicial subordinates ostensibly increases the power of judges within courthouses by increasing the number of staff personnel under the presumptive supervision and control of the judges. The expansion of support staff, however, creates risks that judges will delegate substantive decision-making responsibility to subordinates and fail to adequately supervise staff members' influence over judicial outcomes. Staff members may contribute to these problems through well-intentioned efforts to alleviate the judges' workload burdens and thereby exacerbate bureaucratization problems, especially in regard to Social Security cases, prisoners' cases, paupers' petitions, and other burdensome categories of repetitive filings. According to John Oakley,

[C]ertain kinds of cases may be treated by staff in a routine fashion with inadequate attention to actual merit. This may occur with the best of intentions because the perception of their role by bureaucratic participants leads them to view and describe cases in a way that minimizes [the cases'] novelty and maximizes [the cases'] apparent suitability for staff-generated bureaucratic disposition.[103]

As illustrated by the examples in this chapter, although it is difficult to measure their precise impact, bureaucratizing influences have affected aspects of judicial decision making in trial and appellate courts. These developments create risks that the impact of bureaucratic decision making within the judicial branch is broader than anyone recognizes and could expand in conjunction with continued caseload growth and judicial officers' self-interested denials, and perhaps self-deception, that a serious problem yet exists.

The most interesting question may be whether or not large numbers of judges will ever determine and acknowledge that judicial bureaucratization has ceased to be a mere risk and has become an actual problem. Inevitably, judges will continue to find themselves trapped between their need to admit systemic weaknesses in order to gain resources and their desire to reassure the public that the judiciary is uniquely dependable among the branches of government in fulfilling its responsibilities properly. It is far easier to acknowledge potential problems with the judicial system generally than to admit that problems might be developing within the judges' own decision-making processes. Individual judges, such as Judge Edwards and Judge Rubin, have sounded an alarm about the risks of bureaucratization. Because the scope of the detrimental effects or the risks of such effects upon judicial decision making is defined by the unmeasurable aggregation of impacts in individual courthouses and judges' chambers, the public warnings emanating from individual judges have limited remedial impact. Monitoring judicial decision making for potential problems requires introspection and effort by individual judges throughout the country. However, forthright admissions about internal problems, especially problems under the judges' responsibility and control, can clash with judges' traditional protectiveness of both the judicial branch's image and their own self-image as authority figures whose decisions are principled and proper.

NOTES

1. See, e.g., Owen M. Fiss, "The Bureaucratization of the Judiciary," *Yale Law Journal* 92 (1983): 1442–1468; Patrick E. Higginbotham, "Bureaucracy—The Carcinoma of the Federal Judiciary," *Alabama Law Review* 31 (1980): 261–272; Alvin B. Rubin, "Bureaucratization of the Federal Courts: The Tension Between Justice and Efficiency," *Notre Dame Lawyer* 55 (1980): 648–659.

2. Wade H. McCree, Jr., "Bureaucratic Justice: An Early Warning," *University of Pennsylvania Law Review* 129 (1981): 797.

3. Roger H. Davidson and Walter J. Oleszek, *Congress and Its Members*, 2d ed. (Washington, D.C.: Congressional Quarterly Press, 1985), 240–259.

4. Robert A. Carp and Ronald Stidham, *The Federal Courts*, 2d ed. (Washington, D.C.: Congressional Quarterly Press, 1991), 65–70.

5. Charles T. Goodsell, *The Case for the Bureaucracy* (Chatham, N.J.: Chatham House, 1983), 1.

6. Jack Plano and Milton Greenberg, *The American Political Dictionary* (New York: Holt, Rinehart and Winston, 1962), 175.

7. "The Federal Civil Justice System," *Bureau of Justice Statistics Bulletin* (July 1987), 4; Administrative Office of the U.S. Courts, *Annual Report of the Director of the Administrative Office of the U.S. Courts* (Washington, D.C.: Government Printing Office, 1990), 133.

8. See Tom R. Tyler, *Why People Obey the Law* (New Haven, Conn.: Yale University Press, 1990).

9. Fiss, 1443.

10. Wolf Heydebrand and Carroll Seron, *Rationalizing Justice: The Political Economy of Federal District Courts* (Albany: State University of New York Press, 1990), 134.

11. Ibid., 134–136.

12. Harry T. Edwards, "The Rising Work Load and Perceived 'Bureaucracy' of the Federal Courts: A Causation-Based Approach to the Search for Appropriate Remedies," *Iowa Law Review* 68 (1983): 880.

13. Lawrence Baum, *The Supreme Court*, 4th ed. (Washington, D.C.: Congressional Quarterly Press, 1992), 111.

14. Ibid.

15. Marcia Coyle, "The High Court's Center Falls Apart," *National Law Journal*, 23 August 1993, S1–S5, S15–S22.

16. Harry T. Edwards, "A Judge's View on 'Justice, Bureaucracy, and Legal Method,' " *Michigan Law Review* 80 (1981): 262.

17. H. W. Perry, Jr., "Agenda Setting and Case Selection," in John B. Gates and Charles A. Johnson, eds., *The American Courts: A Critical Assessment*, 236 (Washington, D.C.: Congressional Quarterly Press, 1991).

18. David M. O'Brien, *Storm Center: The Supreme Court in American Politics*, 2d ed. (New York: W. W. Norton, 1990), 223.

19. Ibid., 165.

20. Ibid., 165–167.

21. Administrative Office of the U.S. Courts, 103.

22. See Christopher E. Smith, "Examining the Boundaries of *Bounds*: Prison Law Libraries and Access to the Courts," *Howard Law Journal* 30 (1987): 27–44.

23. Gideon v. Wainwright, 372 U.S. 335 (1963); see Anthony Lewis, *Gideon's Trumpet* (New York: Random House, 1964).

24. D. Marie Provine, *Case Selection in the United States Supreme Court* (Chicago: University of Chicago Press, 1980), 44–45.

25. William C. Louthan, *The United States Supreme Court: Lawmaking in the Third Branch of Government* (Englewood Cliffs, N.J.: Prentice-Hall, 1991), 14, citing Bob Woodward and Scott Armstrong, *The Brethren: Inside the Supreme Court* (New York: Simon and Schuster, 1979), 33–34.

26. Ibid.

27. William H. Rehnquist, "Another View: Clerks Might 'Influence' Some Actions," *U.S. News & World Report*, 21 February 1958, 116. See also William H. Rehnquist, "Who Writes Decisions of the Supreme Court?" *U.S. News & World Report*, 13 December 1957, 74–75.

28. See Rubin, 652; Edwards, "A Judge's View," 260, 263–266.

29. "Chief Justice's 1991 Year-End Report on the Federal Judiciary," *Third Branch* 24 (January 1992): 2.

30. William H. Rehnquist, *The Supreme Court: How It Was, How It Is* (New York: William Morrow, 1987), 265–266.

31. Ibid., 26–38.

32. H. W. Perry, Jr., *Deciding to Decide: Agenda Setting in the United States Supreme Court* (Cambridge: Harvard University Press, 1991), 78.

33. O'Brien, 222–223.

34. See, e.g., C. Neal Tate and Roger Handberg, "Time Binding and Theory Building in Personal Attribute Models of Supreme Court Voting Behavior, 1916–88," *American Journal of Political Science* 35 (1991): 460–480; James L. Gibson, "From Simplicity to Complexity: The Development of Theory in the Study of Judicial Behavior," *Political Behavior* 5 (1983): 7–49.

35. Provine, 23.

36. Saul Brenner and Jan Palmer, "The Law Clerks' Recommendations and Chief Justice Vinson's Vote in Certiorari," *American Politics Quarterly* 18 (1990): 68–86.

37. Provine, 25–26.

38. Rehnquist, *The Supreme Court*, 266.

39. *This Honorable Court; Inside the Marble Temple* (documentary film broadcast 12 September 1989 on PBS).

40. Thomas B. Marvell, *Appellate Courts and Lawyers* (Westport, Conn.: Greenwood Press, 1978), 95.

41. Rubin, 651.

42. Joseph Vining, "Justice, Bureaucracy, and Legal Method," *Michigan Law Review* 80 (1981): 251.

43. O'Brien, 161–164.

44. Rehnquist, *The Supreme Court*, 296–301.

45. David J. Brown, "Facing the Monster in the Judicial Closet: Rebutting a Presumption of Sloth," *Judicature* 75 (1992): 291.

46. Administrative Office of the U.S. Courts, 105.

47. Rubin, 650.

48. J. Woodford Howard, *The Courts of Appeals in the Federal Judicial System* (Princeton, N.J.: Princeton University Press, 1981), 198.

49. See, e.g., Joy A. Chapper and Roger A. Hanson, *Intermediate Appellate Courts: Improving Case Processing* (Williamsburg, Va.: National Center for State Courts, 1990), 59.

50. Richard Posner, *The Federal Courts: Crisis and Reform* (Cambridge: Harvard University Press, 1985), 113.

51. John Bilyeu Oakley and Robert S. Thompson, *Law Clerks and the Judicial Process* (Berkeley: University of California Press, 1980), 139.

52. Howard, 279.

53. Ibid.

54. Ibid.

55. Ibid.

56. Ibid.

57. Ibid.

58. Ibid.

59. Ibid., 279–280.

60. Posner, 103.

61. John B. Oakley, "The Screening of Appeals: The Ninth Circuit's Experience in the Eighties and Innovations for the Nineties," *Brigham Young University Law Review* (1991): 864–866.

62. Posner, 112.

63. Donald R. Songer, "Criteria for Publication of Opinions in the U.S. Courts of Appeals: Formal Rules Versus Empirical Reality," *Judicature* 73 (1990): 307–313.

64. Mary Lou Stow and Harold J. Spaeth, "Centralized Research Staff: Is There a Monster in the Judicial Closet?" *Judicature* 75 (1992): 216–221.

65. Ibid., 220.

66. See Brown, 291–293; "Letters," *Judicature* 75 (1992): 288–289.

67. "Stow and Spaeth Respond," *Judicature* 75 (1992): 290.

68. Mary Lou Stow and Harold Spaeth, "Examining an Analogy: Does the Judicial Monster Eat Chaff?" *Judicature* 75 (1992): 294.

69. McCree, 787–789.

70. Ibid., 789.

71. Fiss, 1467.

72. Ibid.

73. Posner, 115.

74. Ibid., 119.

75. Ibid., 104.

76. Ibid., 117.

77. "Chief Justice's 1991 Year-End Report," 2.

78. See, e.g., Judith Resnik, "Managerial Judges," *Harvard Law Review* 96 (1982): 374–448.

79. Rubin, 651.

80. Ibid., 652.

81. See Carroll Seron, "The Professional Project of Parajudges: The Case of U.S. Magistrates," *Law and Society Review* 22 (1988): 557–574.

82. See Peter G. McCabe, "The Federal Magistrates Act of 1979," *Harvard Journal on Legislation* 16 (1979): 343–401.

83. Administrative Office of the U.S. Courts, 24–25.

84. Christopher E. Smith, *United States Magistrates in the Federal Courts: Subordinate Judges* (New York: Praeger, 1990), 115–146.

85. Carroll Seron, *The Roles of Magistrates: Nine Case Studies* (Washington, D.C.: Federal Judicial Center, 1985), 35–46.

86. Ibid.

87. Smith, *United States Magistrates*, 19–20.

88. See Judith Resnik, "The Mythic Meaning of Article III Courts," *University of Colorado Law Review* 56 (1985): 581–617.

89. See Dissenting Views of the Hon. John Seiberling, House Report No. 1364, Magistrates Act of 1978, 95th Cong., 2d Sess. (1978), 40–41.

90. Smith, *United States Magistrates*, 131.

91. Ibid., 178–180.

92. Seron, 61.

93. Smith, *United States Magistrates*, 180.

94. Christopher E. Smith, "From U.S. Magistrates to U.S. Magistrate Judges: Developments Affecting the Federal District Courts' Lower Tier of Judicial Officers," *Judicature* 75 (1992): 212–214.

95. See Christopher E. Smith, "The Development of a Judicial Office: United States Magistrates and the Struggle for Status," *Journal of the Legal Profession* 14 (1989): 175–197.

96. See William Bennett Turner, "When Prisoners Sue: A Study of Prisoner Section 1983 Suits in the Federal Courts," *Harvard Law Review* 92 (1979): 610–663; Roger A. Hanson, "What Should Be Done When Prisoners Want to Take the State to Court?" *Judicature* 70 (1987): 223–227.

97. Christopher E. Smith, "United States Magistrates and the Processing of Prisoner Litigation," *Federal Probation* 52 (December 1988): 15.

98. Christopher E. Smith, *Courts and the Poor* (Chicago: Nelson-Hall, 1991), 69.

99. Smith, *United States Magistrates*, 175.

100. See Christopher E. Smith, "Assessing the Consequences of Judicial Innovation: U.S. Magistrates' Trials and Related Tribulations," *Wake Forest Law Review* 23 (1988): 483–488.

101. See Oakley and Thompson, 27–28.

102. Smith, *United States Magistrates*, 187.

103. Oakley, "The Screening of Appeals," 875.

6

Conclusion

When federal judges use their powers to decide cases that overtly shape public policy, they can generate controversy and political opposition.[1] Judicial decisions on school desegregation, abortion, prayer in school, and other issues produced broad recognition of federal judges' role as influential policy makers within the American governing system. Judges' influence is less obvious, however, when applied to procedures and policies affecting court administration. Although less visible to the public, judges' influence over court administration is significant because court procedures and practices affect the outcomes produced by the judicial process.

Judges' power over formal judicial policy making and their influence over court administration are different in important respects. For example, as mentioned above, formal judicial decisions and their consequences are more visible and recognized than judges' influence over court procedures and practices. A particularly important difference between judges' power over formal policy decisions and their influence on reform of court procedures concerns the judges' motivations for action. In formal judicial decision making, judges' decisions are based on personal political values, judicial philosophies, and legal arguments presented by the litigants as judges try to determine the "best" solution for the legal conflict presented in a case.[2] The judges may have no personal involvement or stake in the particular issue that they must decide, but they seek to achieve the "best" outcome according to their values and interpretive methods.

By contrast, judges' actions to influence court administration are affected by the judges' personal self-interest in maintaining their status, authority, independence, and accoutrements of judicial office. Judges frequently justify their actions by saying, and indeed probably they genuinely believe, that they are motivated entirely by a sincere desire to do whatever is "best" for the federal court system. For example, as illustrated by the chapter on judicial salaries, the judges made arguments about the harm to the court system from their stagnant salaries, but close examination revealed that they failed to substantiate their claims that federal judges were leaving the bench as a result of dissatisfaction with salaries. Indeed, their arguments concerning their "poverty"[3] and their "inability" to send their children to college[4] revealed more about their myopia and insulation from mainstream American society than about any widespread problem in the judicial branch. What the judges deem to be "best" for the judicial system when they advocate or oppose specific reforms seldom, if ever, involves a reduction in their own power, status, and autonomy.

The judges' identification of the judicial system's best interests with the judges' self-interest is not surprising because many federal judges view themselves as the personal embodiment of the judicial branch of government. This conceptualization was evident in studies of the U.S. magistrate judges' role in the federal judicial system:

Judges who evinced a willingness to use the magistrates broadly tended to view themselves and the magistrates [as] working for a common enterprise — the federal courts. By contrast, judges who limited magistrates' activities frequently spoke as if they embodied the federal court and therefore the magistrates' purpose was to assist them personally.[5]

Even judges who see themselves as working for the courts, rather than embodying the judicial branch, may not be able to separate their self-interest from other considerations in deciding how to shape and implement court procedures. Thus, just as some corporate interests have operated under a premise aptly captured in the statement "What's good for General Motors is good for America," many federal judges appear to be motivated by the belief that "What's good for federal judges is good for the court system."

Manifestations of self-interest are not inherently improper or harmful. In fact, they are usually inevitable when human beings possess the power, opportunity, means, and motivation to improve their resources, status, or power. However, when manifested by federal judges, especially those who may blindly accept that their interests are identical to those of the judicial branch, there are grave risks that judges' manifestations of self-interest will produce undesirable consequences. As illustrated by the chapters on judicial bureaucracy and habeas corpus reform, judges' interests in combatting the pressures of burdensome caseloads have produced, respectively, threats to careful, considered judgments within judicial decision making and to the quality of justice produced in the criminal process.

JUDGES AND COURT REFORM LEGISLATION

When judges engage in formal judicial policy making, they are not independently authoritative and effective. They can pronounce formal decisions concerning controversial issues, but they are dependent on other branches of government to implement those decisions.[6] If citizens disobey judicial decisions and officials in the legislative and executive branches of government do not act to enforce compliance, then judicial policy making may be merely symbolic. For example, despite all of the public attention to the Supreme Court's landmark decision against racial segregation in *Brown v. Board of Education* (1954), Gerald Rosenberg found that little significant desegregation took place until a decade later when Congress and the executive branch actively began to use their powers to implement desegregation.[7] Thus judges control formal policy pronouncements, but are dependent on other branches of government for the implementation of their decisions. By contrast, when proposals emerge that concern reform of court administration, federal judges are dependent on Congress for the development of the formal enactments, but the judges have significant control over the implementation of any practices and procedures mandated by the legislative process.

The judges are on different footing than many other interest groups when they try to influence the shape of legislative enactments. Decisions and actions by members of Congress are primarily motivated by their desire to gain reelection. Although Richard Fenno, Jr., has argued that members of Congress also seek to achieve influence within Congress and make "good" public policy,[8] David Mayhew has rightly noted that reelection "has to be the *proximate* goal of everyone, the goal that must be achieved over and over if other ends are to be entertained. . . . Reelection underlies everything else."[9] Unlike other interest groups who can offer legislators financial and electoral support, federal judges have little to offer that will contribute to the overriding reelection goal of members of Congress. Federal judges must use alternative means to influence Congress.

Although federal judges cannot influence Congress through campaign contributions, grassroots lobbying, and the other techniques of interest groups, they benefit from various resources and their relationships with members of Congress. For example, as indicated in the chapter on the Judicial Improvements Act, the judges often find themselves enjoying what David Truman once characterized as "the defensive advantage" in the legislative process.[10] Because judges seek to preserve the significant authority and status that they already possess, the advocates of change bear the greatest burden for moving Congress to take action to reform the federal court system. It is frequently easier to delay, obstruct, or weaken legislative proposals than to push a new bill through the legislative process toward enactment. In their defensive posture, judges can sound the alarm about the potential detrimental consequences of any legislative proposals that might threaten their autonomy and accoutrements of judicial office. The judges' arguments will naturally focus on aspects of reform proposals that potentially threaten the effectiveness of the federal court system rather than acknowledge that the judges' personal self-interest is at issue. Many members of Congress may prefer to maintain the status quo, even with recognized problems, rather than risk initiating reforms that might create new or different problems.

Unlike issues of concern to other political interests, judicial administration issues often have little low visibility and are not salient to political parties or the public. Specific judicial issues may generate political attention and conflict because they threaten the interests of influential institutions or actors. For example, proposals to expand the number of federal judgeships invariably attract scrutiny from one political party if the opposing political party controls the White House and will be able to fill those new judgeships with supportive partisans. Similarly, the original proposal to divide the Fifth Circuit Court of Appeals into two circuits attracted the attention of worried civil rights advocates,[11] and proposals to cap jury awards for medical practices lawsuits generate opposition from the plaintiff bar.[12] In these instances, court reform proposals attract attention by threatening the interests of specific groups that possess organizational resources. By contrast, other kinds of legislative proposals affecting court procedures and resources are of little interest to the public or mobilized interest groups.

Although there are more than 700,000 lawyers in the United States, the actual "policy community," in John Kingdon's terminology, of individuals concerned with issues of court procedure is quite small.[13] Civil justice reform and bureaucratization of the judiciary will affect case processing and case outcomes, but these developments do not have a clear and direct impact on any particular interest groups possessing organizational resources—except for the federal judges. Specific lawyers' organizations take an interest in such issues, but their interest is unlikely to mobilize members of the legal profession to undertake widespread lobbying activities. Moreover, mainstream lawyers' organizations consistently defer to and support the preferences of judges on many court reform issues. This is not surprising, since lawyers and judges, who are former lawyers, share a common socialization with its attendant implications for shared values and perspectives on the judicial process. In addition, the judges are authoritative decision makers whose decisions and relationships with lawyers affect the success and profitability of attorneys' law firms. Thus there are few impediments to federal judges influencing developments concerning court reform issues that received legislative attention when the opposition consists only of individual members of Congress and judicial reformers rather than mobilized interests with the resources necessary to direct traditional lobbying pressures and incentives at legislators. It is, of course, far more difficult for the judges themselves to initiate issues and ensure that those issues actually receive legislative attention.

As Deborah Barrow and Thomas Walker found in their study of the creation of the Eleventh Circuit Court of Appeals, court reform develops through a process of "cooperative oversight" in which a generally disinterested or distracted Congress defers to the recommendations of federal judges. According to Barrow and Walker, this "pragmatic policy arrangement . . . accommodates the constitutional responsibility of Congress to oversee the lower courts while supporting the integrity and independence of the judiciary."[14] Congressional deference is fed not only by respect for considerations of separation of powers and the need for an independent judiciary, but also by a natural and respectful regard for the expertise of the judicial professionals who work with court procedures and practices every day. For example, with respect to the Judicial Improvements Act, Senator Joseph Biden had the opportunity to push ahead with original proposals despite the opposition of federal judges and U.S. magistrates. In reality, however, it would have been difficult for him to persuade other members of Congress to support his original proposals without some compelling reason for overriding the federal judges' objections. In order to advance his objectives, Senator Biden had few realistic alternatives other than to compromise by working closely with and accommodating the judges in order to produce legislation that took a first step toward his goal of developing innovative civil litigation procedures.

Other factors also contribute to the cooperative oversight model of federal court reform. Federal judges are drawn from political elites who frequently have preexisting relationships with members of Congress. In addition, Barrow and Walker found that judges had relationships with congressional staff, particularly through former judicial law clerks who later took positions on congressional committees.[15] Such personnel exchanges between interest groups and government subunits often provide the basis for interest influence over the agency or committee.[16] In addition, lawyers are disproportionately overrepresented in Congress. For example, 251 of 535 members of the Ninety-Ninth Congress were lawyers.[17] The common education and socialization experiences of lawyers appear to enhance their automatic support for and deference to the judgments of their profession's leaders—namely, the judges.[18] Furthermore, the nonlawyers among members of Congress may feel that they lack the knowledge and legitimacy to criticize or question technical proposals affecting a highly specialized branch of the government.

While Barrow and Walker's cooperative oversight model provides a good framework for understanding the politics of judicial reform, it also highlights the risks posed by the normal legislative processes affecting court administration. Because of congressional deference to judges and the connections between Congress and the federal judiciary, no one is well positioned to question the role of judges' self-interest in court administration. For example, while Ralph Nader and a few other gadflies publicly questioned the need for judicial salary increases in 1989, no members of Congress or organized interest groups seriously challenged the basis for and implications of the judges' self-interested arguments.

Judges shape the consequences of legislation because they can determine how court administration procedures will be implemented within their own courthouses. As indicated in the discussion of the Judicial Improvements Act, the fragmentation of power within the judicial branch permits judges to regulate the nature and timing of the implementation of court procedures. The judges may even disregard completely specific aspects of legislation and court rules, as illustrated by the judge cited in Chapter 2 who had his law clerk preside over conferences that were supposed to be under the supervision of judges or magistrates. The fragmentation of power and the autonomy of federal judges have been applied to alter or weaken various court reform initiatives, including, for example, the Speedy Trial Act.[19] Unlike in formal judicial policy making, in which the judiciary is dependent on the legislative and executive branches for implementing new policies, the shoe is on the other foot when it comes to court administration.

The judges' power over implementation has two consequences. First, the judges need not win complete "victories" in their efforts to shape court reform legislation. As long as the legislation is not too strong, too explicit, or too well known, the judges can subvert aspects of legislative enactments with which they disagree. Technically, judges run the risk of having cases overturned on appeal if they do not follow legislative requirements and court rules precisely. In reality, however, lawyers and litigants often do not know all of the details of court rules, so they do not recognize when federal judges are subverting proper procedures. For example, magistrate judges in one district presided over civil consent trials in clear violation of a congressional statute because their supervising judges had never certified that they were qualified to preside over such trials. Local lawyers, however, never challenged the magistrate judges' authority because they had no idea that the judges and magistrate judges were violating a technical aspect of the Magistrates Act of 1979.[20] Moreover, lawyers have a disincentive to challenge judges' practices because they know that they will be presenting cases to these same federal judges in the future and they would prefer, if at all possible, to maintain favorable relationships with the judges. Such relationships may be threatened if a lawyer, in effect, accuses a judge of intentionally violating a statute or court rule.

A second consequence of judges' control over implementation is that realists among members of Congress may recognize the need for cooperation with the judges in order to avoid the likelihood that judges will find ways to ignore or subvert legislative enactments with which they disagree.

As indicated by the discussion of habeas corpus reform, judges possess a huge advantage not possessed by other interest groups: They may have the opportunity to bypass the legislature and use their authoritative positions to impose new rules and procedures. Many of the Supreme Court's decisions affecting habeas corpus procedures do not involve any interpretation of either the Constitution or habeas corpus statutes. Supreme Court justices have simply asserted, without challenge from Congress, the authority to create and change rules for habeas corpus petitions. When the group disadvantaged by the judicially initiated court reforms is small, politically powerless, and, in the case of prisoners, despised, there is virtually no incentive for legislators to use their political resources to constrain court decisions affecting judicial reform. The assertion of so-called inherent judicial powers over issues affecting the courts gives federal judges special opportunities to advance their goals while simultaneously creating serious risks that judicial officers will not recognize the implications and consequences of their pursuit of perceived self-interest. In the example of habeas corpus reform, the justices creating the reforms apparently do not recognize the risks of unjust outcomes, or they believe, as Justice Antonin Scalia does, that governors will correct injustices through sentence commutations and pardons.[21] These justices also do not accurately perceive the unanticipated burdens they place on district courts by forcing initial decision makers (e.g., magistrate judges, law clerks, *pro se* clerks) to address additional procedural issues in processing habeas petitions.

As indicated by the foregoing discussion, in spite of their inability to use traditional interest-group strategies for threatening or reinforcing legislators' goal of winning reelection, federal judges possess relationships and resources that permit them to assert significant influence over court reform issues that are ostensibly under congressional control. This does not mean that judges can always attain their desired goals. As indicated by the chapter on judicial salaries, it can be difficult for judges to *initiate* legislative enactments unless they can persuade Congress that a "crisis" exists. However, judges are well positioned to assert their self-interest in reacting to, shaping, and implementing legislative proposals that will affect court administration.

JUDICIAL SELF-INTEREST AND THE FUTURE OF COURT REFORM

Because the judicial branch faces continuing demands for its services from the public, the perception of a caseload "crisis" is likely to feed the judges' inclinations toward self-interested action. As Congress considers proposals to alleviate the caseload burden on the federal courts, the judges will watch closely to ensure that proposed reforms do not threaten their status, autonomy, and power. Moreover, individual judicial officers, especially on the Supreme Court, may continue to seek ways to block access to the courts for specific categories of claimants in order to reduce caseload burdens throughout the system. As illustrated by the examples in Chapter 4, this process will exacerbate risks that judges' self-interested emphasis on efficiency will diminish the supervision of lower court decisions and thereby result in unreliable convictions for serious criminal offenses. If efficiency becomes the predominant value that motivates decisions affecting procedural matters, the justices will have improperly subordinated society's interest in punishing only the genuinely guilty and not the unlucky innocent. Moreover, the justices may inadvertently create new, unanticipated burdens for the district courts that they purport to seek to help.

Because of the federal courts' burdensome caseload, it is difficult to remedy the bureaucratization problem and its attendant consequences. Several possible strategies might lessen, but not eliminate, the current problems. Obviously, greater self-consciousness by judges about the work produced by their subordinates might lead to greater supervision and closer review of law clerks', staff attorneys', and magistrate judges' recommendations. This degree of self-consciousness would require judges to combat their own self-interest in delegating and routinizing decision making, especially for categories of cases that are considered repetitive and less interesting than most cases. Unless caseloads are reduced, however, the same pressure will continue to exist that diminished judges' capacities for supervising staff in the first place. Justice Scalia, Chief Justice William Rehnquist, and others seek to reduce the number of cases filed in federal court in order to ease the pressures that generate bureaucratization.[22] However, this remedy may only make matters worse for the state courts that must handle any categories of cases (e.g., civil suits between residents of different states) that may at some point completely be denied access to the federal courts. This remedy also has consequences for the availability and quality of judicial review for death penalty and other serious cases.

It is unrealistic to expect that federal judges can be selfless when reacting to court administration issues that may affect their status, authority, and autonomy. Their black judicial robes do not erase the powerful human inclinations that lead them to seek the preservation and enhancement of their privileged positions in the American governing system. Although greater self-consciousness by federal judges is desirable, it is not the only mechanism for monitoring and moderating potential detrimental consequences. Legislators can take a more active and less deferential role in court reform.

In the Judicial Improvements Act discussed in Chapter 2, Senator Biden did not achieve his original objective of implementing the Brookings Institution Task Force recommendations, but his sustained attention to court reform forced the federal judiciary to respond to his proposals and negotiate with him about the content of the ultimate legislation. The concept of separation of powers requires that members of Congress respect judicial officers, but it does require that they defer to judges on judicial matters. Article III of the Constitution explicitly grants to Congress the power to determine the structures and processes of the federal judiciary, except with respect to the existence of the United States Supreme Court. Legislators should view critically the claims of federal judges about court administration and actively solicit alternative viewpoints from interested students of judicial affairs in academia and interest groups. Fundamentally, federal judges should be pressed to persuade legislators about the accuracy of their views about court administration problems, desirable reforms, and the probable consequences of such reforms. As indicated by the unintended consequences of habeas corpus reform, legislators should not automatically presume that Supreme Court justices and other leaders of the federal judiciary can accurately anticipate the consequences of court reform.

The examples discussed in the chapters of this book provide several important lessons for students of judicial politics and court reform. First, federal judges shape policy and outcomes not only through formal judicial policy making, but also through their behavior as a political interest group seeking to shape and implement court reform in ways that maintain their own status and authority. Second, analysts must look carefully at judges' claims about the needs and "best interests" of the judicial branch because such claims will frequently obscure the judges' self-interested personal motivations for preserving and enhancing their own positions in the system. Third, because Congress possesses formal authority over court reform legislation, legislators should actively question judges' arguments (e.g., concerning judicial salaries), monitor the consequences of judicial decisions affecting court procedures (e.g., habeas corpus reform), and examine the consequences of judicial control over court reform implementation (e.g., judicial bureaucratization). Congressional cooperation with judicial officers concerning matters affecting court reform has functional benefits for the governing system by avoiding undue legislative interference in and conflict with the independent judicial branch. However, excessive deference to federal judges amounts to abdication of the Congress's Article III responsibilities for designing and maintaining the federal court system. This is especially true when the self-interested quality of federal judges' arguments and actions remains unrecognized and, moreover, may contribute to risks of unjust outcomes (e.g., habeas corpus reform), usurpation of legislative authority (e.g., habeas corpus reform), and excessive routinization of judicial decision making (e.g., judicial bureaucratization). Article III of the Constitution created a system in which federal judges were given the political insulation necessary to make courageous, independent decisions. Because federal judges' significant authority is insulated from many direct forms of political accountability, there are strong reasons for monitoring the manifestations and consequences of self-interest in court reform and judicial administration.

Judicial self-interest should be recognized as both inevitable and, at times, beneficial in protecting and maintaining the resources of the judicial branch. However, judges must be encouraged to develop greater self-consciousness and caution about their own self-interest and its consequences. Moreover, legislators must moderate detrimental risks of judicial self-interest by paying closer attention to the problems facing the judiciary and actively responding in a careful manner to judicial needs. By being more attentive to the resource problems facing the judiciary and by overseeing judicial administration in a more critical and less deferential fashion, Congress, with the assistance of input from scholars and interested groups, may be able to moderate the potentially detrimental risks attendant to manifestations of judicial self-interest.

NOTES

1. See Lino Graglia, *Disaster by Decree* (Ithaca, N.Y.: Cornell University Press, 1976); Donald Horowitz, *The Courts and Social Policy* (Washington, D.C.: Brookings Institution, 1977); Richard E. Morgan, *Disabling America: The "Rights Industry" in Our Time* (New York: Basic Books, 1984); Jeremy Rabkin, *Judicial Compulsion: How Public Law Distorts Public Policy* (New York: Basic Books, 1989).

2. See Lee Epstein and Joseph Kobylka, *The Supreme Court and Legal Change: Abortion and the Death Penalty* (Chapel Hill: University of North Carolina Press, 1992).

3. Committee on the Judicial Branch of the Judicial Conference of the United States, *Simple Fairness: The Case for Equitable Compensation of the Nation's Federal Judges* (Washington, D.C.: Administrative Office of the U.S. Courts, 1988), 31.

4. Press conference of William H. Rehnquist, Washington, D.C. (15 March 1989) (audiotape of C–SPAN broadcast).

5. Christopher E. Smith, *United States Magistrates in the Federal Courts: Subordinate Judges* (New York: Praeger, 1990), 118. See also Carroll Seron, "The Professional Project of Parajudges: The Case of U.S. Magistrates," *Law and Society Review* 22 (1988): 559–563.

6. See Charles A. Johnson and Bradley C. Canon, *Judicial Policies: Implementation and Impact* (Washington, D.C.: Congressional Quarterly Press, 1984).

7. Gerald Rosenberg, *The Hollow Hope: Can Courts Bring About Social Change?* (Chicago: University of Chicago Press, 1991), 46–54.

8. Richard F. Fenno, Jr., *Congressmen in Committees* (Boston: Little, Brown, 1973), 1.

9. David R. Mayhew, *Congress: The Electoral Connection* (New Haven, Conn.: Yale University Press, 1974), 16.

10. David B. Truman, *The Governmental Process: Political Interests and Public Opinion*, 2d ed. (New York: Alfred A. Knopf, 1971), 353.

11. See Deborah J. Barrow and Thomas G. Walker, *A Court Divided: The Fifth Circuit Court of Appeals and the Politics of Judicial Reform* (New Haven, Conn.: Yale University Press, 1988).

12. See Philip J. Hilts, "Bush Enters Malpractice Debate with Plan to Limit Court Awards," *New York Times*, 13 May 1991, A1, A12.

13. John W. Kingdon, *Agendas, Alternatives, and Public Policies* (Boston: Little, Brown, 1984), 123.

14. Barrow and Walker, 249.

15. Ibid., 260–261.

16. Kay Lehman Schlozman and John T. Tierney, *Organized Interests and American Democracy* (New York: Harper & Row, 1986), 341–342.

17. Roger Davidson and Walter Oleszek, *Congress and Its Members*, 2d ed. (Washington, D.C.: Congressional Quarterly Press, 1985), 110.

18. Mark C. Miller, "Lawyers in Congress: What Difference Does It Make?" *Congress & the Presidency* 20 (1993): 1–23.

19. See Malcolm M. Feeley, *Court Reform on Trial* (New York: Basic Books, 1983).

20. Smith, 76.

21. Herrera v. Collins, 113 S. Ct. 853 (1993) (Scalia, J., concurring).

22. See, e.g., Stuart Taylor, "Scalia Proposes Major Overhaul of U.S. Courts," *New York Times*, 16 February 1987, 1, 12.

Selected Bibliography

Barrow, Deborah J., and Thomas G. Walker. *A Court Divided: The Fifth Circuit Court of Appeals and the Politics of Judicial Reform*. New Haven, Conn.: Yale University Press, 1988.

Berry, Jeffrey M. *The Interest Group Society*. Boston: Little, Brown, 1984.

Bok, Derek. *The Cost of Talent: How Executives and Professionals Are Paid and How It Affects America*. New York: Free Press, 1993.

Brenner, Saul, and Jan Palmer. "The Law Clerks' Recommendations and Chief Justice Vinson's Vote in Certiorari." *American Politics Quarterly* 18 (1990): 68–86.

Brookings Institution Task Force. *Justice for All: Reducing Costs and Delay in Civil Litigation*. Washington, D.C.: Brookings Institution, 1989.

Committee on the Judicial Branch of the Judicial Conference of the United States. *Simple Fairness: The Case for Equitable Compensation of the Nation's Federal Judges*. Washington, D.C.: Administrative Office of the U.S. Courts, 1988.

Faust, Richard, Tina J. Rubenstein, and Larry W. Yackle. "The Great Writ in Action: Empirical Light on the Federal Habeas Corpus Debate." *New York University Review of Law and Social Change* 18 (1990–1991): 637–710.

Federal Courts Study Committee. *Report of the Federal Courts Study Committee*. Washington, D.C.: Administrative Office of the U.S. Courts, 1990.

Feeley, Malcolm M. *Court Reform on Trial*. New York: Basic Books, 1983.

Fish, Peter G. *The Politics of Federal Judicial Administration*. Princeton, N.J.: Princeton University Press, 1973.

Fiss, Owen M. "The Bureaucratization of the Judiciary." *Yale Law Journal* 92 (1983): 1442–1468.

Greenberg, Paul E., and James A. Haley. "The Role of the Compensation Structure in Enhancing Judicial Quality." *Journal of Legal Studies* 15 (1986): 417–426.

Heydebrand, Wolf, and Carroll Seron. *Rationalizing Justice: The Political Economy of the Federal District Courts*. Albany: State University Press of New York, 1990.

Katzman, Robert A., ed. *Judges and Legislators: Toward Institutional Comity*. Washington, D.C.: Brookings Institution, 1988.

McCabe, Peter G. "The Federal Magistrates Act of 1979." *Harvard Journal on Legislation* 16 (1979): 343–401.

McCree, Wade H., Jr. "Bureaucratic Justice: An Early Warning." *University of Pennsylvania Law Review* 129 (1981): 777–797.

Miller, Mark C. "Lawyers in Congress: What Difference Does It Make?" *Congress & the Presidency* 20 (1993): 1–23.

Oakley, John B. "The Screening of Appeals: The Ninth Circuit's Experience in the Eighties and Innovations for the Nineties." *Brigham Young University Law Review* (1991): 864–866.

O'Brien, David M. *Storm Center: The Supreme Court in American Politics*. 2d ed. New York: W. W. Norton, 1990.

Perry, H. W., Jr. *Deciding to Decide: Agenda Setting in the United States Supreme Court*. Cambridge: Harvard University Press, 1991.

Posner, Richard. *The Federal Courts: Crisis and Reform*. Cambridge: Harvard University Press, 1985.

Provine, D. Marie. *Case Selection in the United States Supreme Court*. Chicago: University of Chicago Press, 1980.

Resnik, Judith. "Managerial Judges." *Harvard Law Review* 96 (1982): 376–448.

Rosenn, Keith S. "The Constitutional Guaranty Against Diminution of Judicial Compensation." *U.C.L.A. Law Review* 24 (1976): 308–350.

Rubin, Alvin B. "Bureaucratization of the Federal Courts: The Tension Between Justice and Efficiency." *Notre Dame Lawyer* 55 (1980): 648–659.

Schlozman, Kay Lehman, and John T. Tierney. *Organized Interests and American Democracy*. New York: Harper & Row, 1986.

Seron, Carroll. "The Professional Project of Parajudges: The Case of the U.S. Magistrates." *Law and Society Review* 22 (1988): 557–574.

Smith, Christopher E. *United States Magistrates in the Federal Courts: Subordinate Judges*. New York: Praeger, 1990.

———. "Assessing the Consequences of Judicial Innovation: U.S. Magistrates' Trials and Related Tribulations." *Wake Forest Law Review* 23 (1988): 455–490.

Steamer, Robert. *Chief Justice: Leadership and the Supreme Court*. Columbia: University of South Carolina Press, 1986.

Stow, Mary Lou, and Harold J. Spaeth. "Centralized Research Staff: Is There a Monster in the Judicial Closet?" *Judicature* 75 (1992): 216–221.

Stumpf, Harry P. *American Judicial Politics*. San Diego, Calif.: Harcourt Brace Jovanovich, 1988.

Thomas, Jim. "The 'Reality' of Prisoner Litigation: Repackaging the Data." *New England Journal on Criminal and Civil Confinement* 15 (1989): 27–53.

Truman, David B. *The Governmental Process: Political Interests and Public Opinion*. 2d ed. New York: Alfred A. Knopf, 1971.

Van Tassel, Emily Field. *Why Judges Resign: Influences on Federal Judicial Service, 1798 to 1992*. Washington, D.C.: Federal Judicial Center, 1993.

Yackle, Larry. "The Habeas Hagioscope." *Southern California Law Review* 66 (1993): 2231–2431.

Index

About the Author

CHRISTOPHER E. SMITH is Associate Professor in the School of Criminal Justice at Michigan State University. He is the author of 11 books, including *Justice Antonin Scalia and the Supreme Court's Conservative Moment* (Praeger, 1993) and *Critical Judicial Nominations and Political Change* (Praeger, 1993).

ISBN 0-275-95216-9

90000>

EAN

9 780275 952167

HARDCOVER BAR CODE